NORWICH AND THE CIVIL WAR

NORWICH AND THE CIVIL WAR

PATRICIA F. STALEY

THE History PRESS

Published by The History Press
Charleston, SC 29403
www.historypress.net

First published 2015

Manufactured in the United States

ISBN 978.1.62619.992.7

Library of Congress Control Number: 2015944409

For Camden, the newest Staley

and

"In honor of those who served in the war for the Union…that their example may speak to coming generations."

—inscription on the Soldiers' Monument in Guilford, Connecticut

Contents

Preface

In 1861, new soldiers from towns across the state and nation were marching off to war. Some wanted the opportunity to show their patriotism; others felt it was their duty to defend the country against the threat of rebellion; some wanted to "show them Rebs"; and a few went for the pure excitement of the thing.

Norwich, Connecticut, was a wealthy manufacturing town at the confluence of three rivers that provided power to run factory machines and transportation to bring in raw materials and ship out finished products. It was a city filled with men whose names were well known across the country—who could fairly be described as "captains of industry"—but they were largely confined to supporting roles in wartime events. It was the soldiers who became the larger-than-life and heroic figures.

For a small city (population just over fourteen thousand in 1860), Norwich had an extraordinary response to the Civil War. More than 25 percent of the men—and 10 percent of the city's entire population—served in the military.

The city's financial support for the war effort was rapid and generous. Over the first weekend of the war, Norwich raised $20,000 (about $4 million in 2013) in incentives for men who enlisted. A group of 350 women spent the weekend sewing uniforms for the volunteers. Later, the city's women made sure that boxes containing food, clothing, bandages and comfort items went in a steady stream to the soldiers in the field. A year later, additional private funds were raised to provide financial incentives for new recruits.

A map of New London County showing Norwich. *Author's collection.*

As he responded to President Lincoln's call for seventy-five thousand troops, Connecticut governor William A. Buckingham, a Norwich resident, ordered that the volunteers be properly uniformed and equipped—and pledged his personal credit, if needed, to make that happen.

The history of the Civil War has too often been the story of generals giving orders and armies moving from one position to another. The histories of individual regiments provide an entirely new perspective—the war through the eyes of the men who were the "boots on the ground." Stories of individual heroism and sacrifice are abundant and moving.

There have been many books written about the details of the battles, and I leave that aspect of the war to the experts. Likewise, any discussion of Norwich business and industry is left for another day; the firearms factories by themselves could fill a separate volume.

My goal is to tell the little-known stories of the city's soldiers and civilians, the Norwich residents who were involved in all the important events of the war. Connecticut's First and Second Regiments fought under a Norwich division commander at Bull Run; Norwich men fought fiercely at Antietam and stood firm against Pickett's Charge at Gettysburg. They fought at Second Winchester and endured the long confinement at Libby Prison in Richmond, where a Norwich man was among those who tunneled an escape route. A Norwich man volunteered to lead the Forlorn Hope special assault group at Port Hudson, and Norwich men were subjected to the unspeakably harsh conditions and died at Andersonville Prison. They were in the first naval battle at Port Royal, and a Norwich man was in command at the Battle of Fort Fisher to seize the port of Wilmington, North Carolina.

Norwich men led the long column of troops that marched into Richmond and were with Grant as he accepted Lee's surrender at Appomattox. A week later, as the nation mourned its fallen president, Norwich men were in the funeral procession and among the pallbearers.

And a Norwich man became acting vice president of the United States.

This book would not have been possible without the generosity of a number of people who were kind enough to share images and information that proved invaluable. They include: Marianne Vanden Bout, docent at Faith Trumbull Chapter, Daughters of the American Revolution; Vivian Zoe, director of Slater Memorial Museum; Ken and Merrill Keeley, who shared their library of Norwich history publications; Civil War reenactor Penny Havard; the staff at the Connecticut State Library, especially Lizette Pelletier, Jeannie Sherman and Christine Pittsley, who went out of their way to be helpful; and Beth Burgess of the Harriet Beecher Stowe Center in Hartford.

John Banks, who writes an outstanding Civil War blog, was generous enough to share his research about Antietam and Captain John McCall. His blog, johnbanks.blogspot.com, is well worth a look.

Barry Wilson of the Norwich Civil War Round Table answered questions, helped with photography and shared photos and information about monuments and veterans' graves at Norwich's Yantic Cemetery.

Many thanks go to the staff at Otis Library in Norwich, especially reference librarian Kathy Wieland. They are the best.

A big thank-you goes to Ray O'Connell, Paul O'Connell and Ron Stoltz of Yantic Fire Engine Company No. 1 for making the archives available to me. The stories of the McCall brothers and Joseph Tracy provided insight into the impact of the war on individual families and those left behind.

And, as always, much gratitude is due to my family for their love and support.

1

Moving Toward War

Divergence of opinion about slavery had been festering the in the United States since colonial times. The Constitution itself legitimizes slavery through its three-fifths clause, despite the nation's founding declaration that all men are created equal. The next fifty years were littered with legislative attempts to maintain a balance of power between slave-state and free-state legislators—the Northwest Ordinance of 1789 was followed by the Missouri Compromise in 1820 and the Compromise of 1850.

The Great Awakening of the 1820s and '30s gave the abolitionist movement a foothold in the national awareness, in part because of religious leaders and partially because of public figures like William Lloyd Garrison and his newspaper the *Liberator*.

Yet for every person who espoused the antislavery cause, someone else was against it, for reasons that spanned the spectrum from laissez-faire to the paternalistic concern for the slaves to active participation in and support for the slave trade.

During the nineteenth century, Norwich, Connecticut, was an important manufacturing and transportation center and the home of many well-known wealthy industrialists whose mills were located in or near the city. Some of the city's residents—such as General Daniel P. Tyler, Connecticut governor William A. Buckingham, U.S. senator Lafayette S. Foster and industrialist John Fox Slater—were players on the national stage. But it was generally the less well known among the city's residents who were at the center of the major events of the Civil War.

Norwich had strong connections to some of the national events that increased the tensions over slavery. The conflict over Prudence Crandall's attempt to educate African American girls occurred in the neighboring town of Canterbury. Norwich attorney Lafayette Foster was among the lawyers who aided in her defense when she was tried. Aaron Dwight Stevens, a former Norwich resident, was John Brown's second in command at Harper's Ferry in 1859.

Like the rest of the country, Norwich was caught up in the debate over slavery. There were very real economic implications, since much of the city's wealth came from textile mills that relied on Southern cotton as their raw material. In addition, white mill hands were concerned that they would be replaced by African Americans who would take their jobs and work for less money.

Many of the ministers in Norwich churches preached against slavery. John P. Gulliver of the Broadway Congregational Church, Hiram P. Arms at First Congregational in Norwich Town and Alvan Bond—and, later, Malcolm MacGregor Dana—at Second Congregational were all well known for their abolitionist sentiments.

Stories were told about violent reactions to early antislavery meetings, including threats against the ministers who preached and broken windows and near-riots where abolitionist speakers appeared.

In a sermon preached on July 4, 1834, Reverend James Dickinson, pastor of Second Congregational Church, declared that the oppression of slavery made having slaves a sin to be immediately repented. Reverend Dickinson's sermon was printed as a pamphlet and widely circulated. Among those who sold the pamphlet was former Norwich resident David Ruggles, who carried it among the wares in his New York City bookshop. Ruggles, the first African American bookseller in the nation, has been called the most visible among conductors on the Underground Railroad. It was Ruggles who helped Frederick Douglass reach freedom.

DAVID RUGGLES

David Ruggles was born on March 15, 1810, in the shoreline town of Lyme, the eldest of eight children. Sometime after David's birth, the family moved to Bean Hill in the northern part of Norwich.

As a youth, David roamed the woods, skated, climbed trees and played at balls and hoops with other boys, both black and white. He was educated at a school run by the Second Congregational Church in Norwich, which used verses from the Bible as the basis for instruction in reading and writing. Later in his life, Ruggles surprised people with the number of verses from the Bible that he could recite.

By the time he turned seventeen, Ruggles was in New York City working as a sailor and a grocer before he opened the bookshop. He began writing antislavery articles and pamphlets for newspapers and began his work with the Underground Railroad. His erudition was considered a testament to the solid education he received in Norwich.

Frederick Douglass, in his autobiography, described his introduction to Ruggles and the role Ruggles played in his life—from sheltering him as a fugitive from slavery to providing him a new start in life.

SENATOR LAFAYETTE S. FOSTER

Norwich voices were heard in the national debate on the questions of the day. In 1854, the state senate chose state representative Lafayette Foster, a politically inclined Norwich lawyer, as U.S. senator from Connecticut.

Foster, a graduate of Brown College (now Brown University), had been the city's mayor and served several terms in the general assembly, where he was twice chosen Speaker of the House of Representatives.

When Foster took his seat in the Senate in 1855, his colleagues included many of the political heavy-hitters of the time, including Jefferson Davis, Simon Cameron, William Seward, Hamilton Fish, Charles Sumner, Benjamin Wade, Stephen A. Douglas, Lyman Trumbull and Sam Houston.

The year before Foster went to Washington, the Senate had passed the Kansas-Nebraska Act, effectively negating the Missouri Compromise, which prohibited slavery in the territories north of 36°30' latitude. That act led to a series of increasingly violent events in Kansas as proslavery and antislavery settlers clashed.

The tensions manifested throughout the nation as the question of slavery reached the floor of the Senate in more than debate. South Carolina congressman Preston Brooks reacted to a speech by Massachusetts senator Charles Sumner by beating him with a cane in the Senate chamber. Senator Sumner was injured badly enough that it was three years before he returned to the Senate in 1856.

The debate over admitting Kansas to the Union, which lasted five years, established Foster as a voice of reason in an increasingly

Senator Lafayette Foster, taken about 1858. *Courtesy of the Library of Congress. LC-DIG-cwpbh-02138.*

acrimonious discussion. Foster made it clear that he opposed slavery but acknowledged the rights of slaveholders under the U.S. Constitution. His reasoned, logical dissection of the arguments and sound, sharp analysis that went to the heart of the matter brought Foster a reputation as a skillful debater who could feel strongly about a position yet make his argument in a calm, courteous manner.

By 1858, Kansas was still waiting to join the Union. The stumbling block was the wording of the state constitution regarding slavery. A constitution proposed by the Lecompton Convention stipulated that "the right of property is before and higher than any constitutional sanction, and the right of the owner of a slave to such slave and its increase is the same and as inviolable as the right of the owner to any property whatever."

Foster emphatically rejected the proposed article, stating, "That section contains a principle which, in my judgment, is false in morals, false in politics, and false in law. I will never vote for the admission of a State into this Union with a provision so obnoxious as that." He branded it "a reproach and a shame to the age in which we live."

MR. LINCOLN COMES TO NORWICH

The issues that had begun to divide the nation as a whole threatened to split Connecticut as well. When William A. Buckingham sought a third term as Connecticut's governor in 1860, former governor Thomas H. Seymour, a Democrat and hero of the Mexican-American War, opposed him. Seymour argued that slavery was protected under the Constitution and to eliminate it would do serious harm to Connecticut businesses that had interests in the South.

Connecticut's Republican Party leaders recognized that the contest would be tight, so they arranged for Illinois congressman Abraham Lincoln to come to Connecticut to campaign. Lincoln's February 27 speech at New York's Cooper Union grabbed the attention of newspapers across the nation as he decimated the constitutional rationale for slavery—and it catapulted him into the forefront of the field of presidential contenders.

The Norwich speech was not originally part of Lincoln's tour. He was scheduled to speak only in Hartford, New Haven and Bridgeport, but Norwich resident Hugh Henry Osgood went to Hartford to invite Lincoln to Norwich. At first, Lincoln declined because his schedule had been set and didn't allow for deviation. Osgood persisted and pointed out that Lincoln could stop in Norwich between Providence and New Haven. Once he had demonstrated it was possible, Lincoln agreed to visit the city.

A high school freshman named Francis Leavens and some of his friends decided to attend the speech at Norwich Town Hall. His account of the speech appeared in Benjamin Tinkham Marshall's *A Modern History of New London County, Connecticut* (1922) with a note that it had never been published. By then, Leavens was president of the Dime Savings Bank in Norwich.

Leavens wrote:

> *One morning in March, 1860, I was standing with three or four of my classmates of the junior* [grade 9] *class in the Norwich Free Academy when one of the older boys of the senior class came up to us and said, "Boys, if you want to hear a regular western stump speaker, go down to the Town Hall tomorrow night." "Who is he?" we asked, and the answer came, "A man from Illinois named Lincoln, and they say he is great."*
>
> *A man from Illinois named Lincoln meant nothing to us. We had never heard of him, but we had heard of stump speakers, though we had not seen or heard one. Buffalo Bill's Wild West Show had not begun to make its annual visits to New England, and none of us had been west. "Stump speaker" sounded good to us and we decided to go.*
>
> *Boys are not apt to be late at anything likely to interest them, and four of us were among the earliest arrivals at the Town Hall. We seated ourselves on the front bench, and when Mr. Lincoln took his place behind the bar that ran along the front of the platform he was not six feet away from us. In fact, when he leaned forward and swung his long arms in gestures it seemed as if we were in danger of being struck.*
>
> *I will not attempt to describe his appearance; that has been done by many who were intimately associated with him, while artists*

Presidential candidate Abraham Lincoln, about 1858. *Courtesy of the Library of Congress. LC-USZ62-16377.*

and sculptors have faithfully portrayed his form and features. I remember that he was dressed in a black suit and that he wore a wide turnover collar and a black silk sailor's tie, both of which were striking and unusual in this region.

At this distance of time I cannot undertake to report what he said, but we four boys sat on that front bench till ten o'clock, our eyes never leaving him, notwithstanding we had to keep our heads raised at an uncomfortable angle as he towered above us. I have heard many famous orators since, but never have I listened to one with such rapt attention, and no one ever made such a deep and lasting impression upon me.

His speech was richly illustrated with stories and was frequently interrupted by vigorous applause...I shall never cease to be thankful that I was permitted to see and hear him.

Governor Buckingham had befriended Lincoln during his previous visit to Connecticut and remained a stalwart supporter of his throughout the war. He was the master of ceremonies as Lincoln spoke in Hartford and accompanied him during the tour around the state. In Norwich, he entertained Lincoln at his Main Street home before the town hall speech. Following the speech, Lincoln attended a reception and then spent the night at the Wauregan House hotel.

Two months later, the Republican Convention nominated Lincoln as its candidate in the presidential election. After the election, Buckingham sent his congratulations to Lincoln and expressed his hope that the president-elect would be able to "execute the laws all over our land in spite of the combinations of the states." He also felt free to urge the appointment of Glastonbury resident Gideon Welles to the presidential cabinet.

2

Connecticut's War Governor

Connecticut governor William A. Buckingham had been watching national events, and by the close of 1860, he was openly saying he believed compromise with the South was impossible. He almost certainly talked about politics and the issues of the day with Senator Foster, whose house on Broadway was a little too far from Buckingham's Main Street residence to call him a neighbor, but their paths crossed frequently in a city of fourteen thousand residents. It's likely that Foster shared with the governor his own belief that the differences between North and South would lead to war.

Buckingham's business acumen and reputation for great personal integrity stood him in good stead during his eight years as governor, a period of great turmoil. Governor Buckingham anticipated the need to train and equip as many as five thousand militiamen. As a merchant and a manufacturer, Buckingham appreciated the need to obtain equipment for soldiers while it was available and before demand increased prices. He directed Connecticut's quartermaster general to start obtaining weapons to replace the militia's Mexican War–era guns and stockpiling knapsacks and other equipment.

Training the new militiamen required officers—preferably, men who themselves had some military training. Perfection in training and equipment would be required, Buckingham told the state's militia commanders. Looking back, it appears that many unqualified men were appointed to key positions in the military, but the nineteenth-century reality was that the governors—especially those in the North—had

Connecticut's war governor William A. Buckingham. *Courtesy of the Faith Trumbull Chapter of the Daughters of the American Revolution.*

few choices. When the Civil War began, there was no large standing army and only a small pool of professional soldiers. State militia training was limited and couldn't duplicate wartime experience.

It had been thirteen years since the Mexican War ended. Many of the army's officers were Southerners who resigned to join the Confederate Army. That left few experienced military men to head the new regiments being formed in the North. Buckingham had to rely on what he knew of the applicants and on the recommendation of others whose judgment he trusted.

He turned to a Norwich man to be commanding officer of the First Connecticut Volunteer Infantry. Daniel P. Tyler was the only professionally trained military man among those who volunteered their services in the first regiment. At sixty-two, his age might have counted against him, but Tyler was a graduate of West Point, an artillery expert and determined to serve. His sole condition in accepting the appointment was that he would draw no salary.

So well did Tyler train the first Connecticut troops that when they reported to Washington, D.C., General Winfield Scott, who called them the best-equipped and best-trained troops he had seen, promptly recommended Tyler's promotion to general of volunteers (as opposed to general in the regular army).

Buckingham was the first governor to pledge his state's support for the war. On April 15, just three days after Confederates fired on Fort Sumter, he sent a letter to the president, writing, "I beg leave to inform you that the government and citizens of this state are loyal to the Union, that they appreciate the effort you are making to hold and possess the property of the United States and will be happy to render any service in their power to enable you to enforce the laws."

Since Connecticut's general assembly was not in session, there was no way to obtain state funds for the uniforms, weapons and other equipment the new soldiers needed. Although he lacked legal authority, Governor Buckingham requested a $50,000 loan from the Thames Bank in Norwich to meet the expense and pledged his personal fortune against the loan. The local bank offered $100,000, a New Haven bank offered $50,000 and several Hartford banks offered $500,000. Within a few days, the governor had $1 million at his disposal.

The governor may have been commander in chief of the state militia, but legally, Connecticut's legislature was in control. Nevertheless, the governor made an immediate call for one thousand men to fill the regiment that was Connecticut's quota of volunteers.

It took less than four days to fill the ranks of the First Regiment. So many men clamored to be allowed to join the militia that the governor made a personal appeal to the secretary of war, who agreed to accept two additional regiments from Connecticut. The Second Connecticut Regiment mustered a few days later, and within three weeks, the Third Connecticut Regiment was on its way to Washington.

When the legislature convened in May, not only did members ratify the governor's actions and vote to have the state assume the debt, but also they appropriated $2 million for the governor's use.

For the next four years, most of the governor's time and attention was consumed by the war effort and the troops. He worked twelve hours a day, seven days a week, at his offices in Hartford and New Haven and at his Norwich home, which became another office. He crisscrossed the state to speak at rallies and town meetings, visited the troops at their encampments as often as possible and attended funerals of the fallen.

In addition to normal state business, Governor Buckingham had to deal with a mountain of correspondence that included requests for military commissions, letters from soldiers at the front, official communications from the Federal government and petitions on every imaginable topic.

The need for soldiers didn't end with the initial enlistments. In the summer of 1861, President Lincoln called for an additional 500,000 volunteers to enlist for three years or the duration of the war. Periodically over the next four years, the War Department assigned to each state its share of the needed number of men.

It is estimated that fifty-five thousand Connecticut men—nearly half of the men between the ages of fifteen and fifty—fought for the Union. They formed thirty infantry regiments, artillery brigades and cavalry units.

The governor's efforts did not go unnoticed at the highest levels. President Lincoln was quoted as saying, "The Connecticut regiments give me no trouble; Governor Buckingham always sends them fully equipped for any emergency."

Despite the many demands on his time, the governor remained committed to overseeing the welfare of Connecticut troops. He was famously quoted as telling one man whose duties kept him at the front, "You will see many battles and much suffering: don't let any Connecticut man suffer for want of anything that can be done for him—if it costs money, draw on me for it."

When Governor Buckingham visited Connecticut troops in the field, he did it both to check on conditions at the camps and because it pleased him to do so.

In *The Military and Civil History of Connecticut During the War of 1861–65*, Crofut and Morris described one scene that occurred, probably about April 1862, when the governor was visiting Connecticut's new First Heavy Artillery Regiment at its camp near Washington.

> *Upon leaving one of their camps,* [Buckingham] *asked: "Well, boys, is there anything else I can do for you?"*
>
> *"If you can hurry up the pay master we shall be obliged to you, for it is a long time since we have seen him," was the answer.*
>
> *"Certainly, I'll see what I can do about it," were his parting words, and they found that before he left he had drawn his personal check for the amount due them.*
>
> *As to providing transportation for those who would seek their sick or wounded friends in the field, or bring home their dead, or furnish those in prison with some comforts, or only give the boys in camp some pleasant remembrances of home life and the Thanksgiving delicacies they used to enjoy there, in all such work the Governor took the liveliest interest, and spared neither trouble nor expense to aid in it.*

During the 1860s, Connecticut elections had importance far beyond the borders of the state. In 1861, Southerners branded Buckingham as "one more Black Republican" whose election would increase the pressure to abolish slavery.

In 1863, the spring election in Connecticut was followed closely by Democrats who thought war-weary voters would favor a peace candidate over a Lincoln ally. Buckingham's potential defeat in Connecticut could foreshadow a loss for Lincoln in the 1864 election.

The Lincoln administration also recognized the importance of the Connecticut election. Secretary of War Edwin M. Stanton sent a letter to the governor, offering any assistance needed for the coming election. The offer was apparently accepted, as Connecticut soldiers were granted furloughs to return home to vote, which undoubtedly tipped the balance in the election. Buckingham's margin of victory—2,400 votes—closely matched the number of furloughed soldiers who came home to cast their ballots.

Connecticut returned the favor early in 1864 when the general assembly changed the state constitution to allow soldiers to vote by absentee ballot.

THE GOVERNOR'S STAFF

For his closest advisors and aides, the governor relied heavily on relatives and personal connections, mainly from Norwich. One photo of Governor Buckingham and his staff shows the governor surrounded by aides who were identified as Colonel William Fitch of Bozrach, paymaster general; Colonel Horace J. Morse of New York, adjutant general; General William A. Aiken of Norwich, quartermaster general; Colonel Hugh Henry Osgood of Norwich, aide-de-camp; Colonel Henry R. Bond of Norwich, aide-de-camp; Colonel Calvin G. Child of Norwich, aide-de-camp; and another aide-de-camp, "Colonel Watson," for whom no first name was given. "Watson" may actually have been Colonel Israel Matson of Old Lyme, whose name appears on an official list of the governor's aides.

Other members of the governor's military staff included Hartford businessman Joseph D. Williams, adjutant general for the first two years of the war; John H. Almy of New York, assistant quartermaster general; and Morris Gates of Norwich, assistant adjutant general.

Williams was succeeded in 1863 by Horace J. Morse of Hartford. Morse, a lawyer by training, was an Ohio native educated at Cambridge University in England. Governor Buckingham commissioned Morse as adjutant general in June 1863. After the war, Morse moved to New York and was an original member of the New York investment firm A.M. Kidder, where he remained until his death sixty-three years later.

Colonel William Fitch was commissioned Connecticut's paymaster general in July 1862. Fitch—a resident of Bozrah, a town adjacent to Norwich—later lived in New Haven.

Governor Buckingham and his military staff, about 1864. *Front row, left to right*: Paymaster General William Fitch; Adjutant General Horace J. Morse; Governor William A. Buckingham; Brigadier General William A. Aiken, quartermaster general; Colonel H.H. Osgood, aide-de-camp. *Back row, left to right*: Lieutenant Colonel Henry R. Bond, aide-de-camp; Lieutenant Colonel Israel Matson, aide-de-camp; Colonel John H. Almy, assistant quartermaster general; Lieutenant Calvin G. Child, aide-de-camp; Colonel Morris P. Gates, assistant adjutant general. *Courtesy of the Connecticut State Library Archives. Connecticut Group Portraits Collection (PG 560).*

William A. Aiken served as quartermaster general of Connecticut from 1862 to the end of the war. He was a wholesale grocer in Chicago for two years before coming to Norwich, arriving in time to be listed in the 1860 city directory.

Calvin Goddard Child was a Norwich boy, the grandson of attorney Calvin Goddard, who had been a congressman and justice of the Connecticut Supreme Court. He was appointed the governor's secretary in May 1862 and became a military aide in August of that year. Colonel Child was a graduate of Yale and Harvard Law School and practiced law in Norwich for the three years between graduation and the start of the war. After the war, he moved to Stamford, where he became U.S. district attorney for Connecticut and maintained a private law practice with clients including the New York and New Haven Railroad.

The governor's cousin Israel Matson of Old Lyme served as an aide for four years, according to a biographical sketch in *Genealogical and Biographical*

Record of New London County, Connecticut. Matson, a farmer, was considered one of the town's leading citizens and served several terms in the state legislature.

Henry Richardson Bond was the son of the Reverend Alvan Bond of Norwich. He was also the governor's nephew by marriage as the husband of Mary Perit Ripley (whose father was James L. Ripley, Mrs. Buckingham's brother). Bond was a merchant, a banker and, after the war, a manufacturer.

Colonel Hugh Henry Osgood. *Courtesy of the Faith Trumbull Chapter of the Daughters of the American Revolution.*

When the war began, another nephew, Henry W. Birge, was a Buckingham aide. He was the son of Mrs. Buckingham's sister, Lucy, and her husband, Backus Birge. Initially, he served with the Fourth Connecticut Regiment but was promoted to commander of the Thirteenth Connecticut Infantry.

The only aide whose service spanned the entire four years of the conflict was Hugh Henry Osgood, a Norwich druggist. After the war, Colonel Osgood became involved in textile manufacturing and was an organizer and first president of Norwich's board of trade and served as mayor of the city.

JOHN H. ALMY

In 1862, Buckingham commissioned John H. Almy as Connecticut's assistant quartermaster general. Almy, an 1855 graduate of Amherst College, held the rank of lieutenant colonel and was paid as a cavalry officer, according to the practice at the time. Since the Almys were a prominent Norwich family, it is likely that the governor knew young Almy well.

Almy went to New York City, where he acted as agent for Connecticut and worked with the city's Sons of Connecticut group to establish the New England Soldiers' Relief Association to oversee the welfare of New England troops coming through New York. Besides feeding troops as they came through New York, the group arranged transportation home for sick and wounded soldiers.

Almy's other duties involved collection of back pay and bounties; correcting errors in passes and descriptive lists; obtaining furloughs; receiving boxes of sanitary goods and forwarding them to the proper destinations; caring for baggage; procuring regimental flags and guidons; obtaining musical instruments for various bands and small arms for officers; arranging discharges for sick and disabled soldiers; and responding to letters inquiring about the missing, sick or dead.

Over four years, Almy's records show more than 200,000 soldiers from Connecticut and other states were served. Of that total, 60,000 were sick and wounded. All received transportation, and many were assisted in other ways. Donations from citizens in Connecticut met only part of the cost of these services; Almy covered the rest from his salary.

In his report to the governor, J.D. Williams, Connecticut's adjutant general for the first half of the war, wrote of Almy, "The sick and wounded soldier returning to his home has always found in him a friend whose sympathies were wrought into practical form, and many an anxious wife, mother or sister has received valuable advice and directions in their efforts for the relief of a suffering husband, son, or brother in the field or hospital."

3

The First Salvos

January 1, 1861

In the nation's capital, guests gathered at the home of Secretary of State William H. Seward for a New Year's dinner party. They included Senator Preston King of New York and Martha Foster, wife of Senator Lafayette S. Foster of Norwich.

When Mrs. Foster stated her belief that the country was "drifting" into civil war, Senator King lightheartedly suggested she had nothing to worry about. Her reply, that her husband shared her opinion, brought a serious question about whether Senator Foster truly believed war was coming. Her affirmative response left King "laugh[ing] heartily at the absurdity of it," joined by Secretary Seward, who "even more strongly ridiculed such a foreboding." Foster was not at the table, as he was away on what a biography described as a "secret mission for the incoming administration."

The War Begins

For some time, the Southern states had threatened to leave the Union if a Republican president was elected in 1860. When the votes were counted, the Republican Abraham Lincoln was declared the winner, and in the next month, five of the Southern states had begun preparations to secede.

Senator Foster found himself in a position where his principles clashed loudly with his commitment to the rule of law. For Foster, the dilemma was that although he was morally opposed to the institution of slavery and absolutely opposed its spread to new territories or into the North, he also believed slavery was recognized in the Constitution and the constitutional guarantees already in place must be respected.

Foster's willingness to compromise to avoid the war he had come to believe was inevitable was strongly criticized in Connecticut. He was, they said, willing to abandon his principles and go to any length to avoid the conflict.

An excerpt from Foster's response to a critical friend was printed in the *Hartford Courant* on January 21, 1861:

> *As to yielding the principles for which I, in common with my political associates, have been contending so long, I certainly have not "backed down"—do not propose to. Disruption of the Union, is, I believe, inevitable. So believing, it does not seem to me desirable to use irritating words, to criminate or recriminate; if disunion be a blessing, we are like to enjoy it. I believe it will lead to war and bloodshed, and I deprecate it. Still, I am opposed to having slavery established or recognized by the constitution of the country beyond the limits or terms originally assigned to it, be the consequences what they may. To found a government on a principle so clearly violative of human right—so offensive to God—must sooner or later call down His curse. It is surely better that we refuse to incorporate this demand into our recognized law, even in view of the most terrible alternative which can be presented. None can be so terrible as the wrath of God, which would surely visit us if we consented to the enormity.*

Over the next four months, Foster could only watch as, one by one, Southern states left the Union, taking with them men he had called colleagues and friends. The Senate seating chart for the Thirty-fifth Congress (1857–59) shows Foster surrounded by Southerners whom he would have come to know well. John Bell of Tennessee sat on his left; Benjamin Fitzpatrick of Alabama and Joseph Evans of South Carolina in front; and Robert Toombs of Georgia and J.P. Benjamin of Louisiana were immediately behind him.

The seating chart for the Thirty-sixth Congress (1859–61) reflected a vastly different seating arrangement. Foster was surrounded by senators from the Northeast and Midwest, all of them Republicans, except for a few Democrats and third-party members. The Southern senators,

Democrats all, had decamped across the aisle, with a only a few free-staters, also Democrats, among them.

SECESSION

During the first half of 1861, the tempo of events moved ever more quickly; it must have seemed that every day's paper brought more bad news. South Carolina had withdrawn from the Union on December 20. Like dominoes, other states quickly followed: Mississippi seceded on January 9, followed by Florida a day later and Alabama the day after that. By the end of January, Georgia and Louisiana had left the Union.

Formation of the Confederate States of America was announced on February 9, and on February 18, 1861, former senator Jefferson Davis was sworn in as president of the Confederacy. On March 2, Texas became the seventh state to secede.

FORT SUMTER

Abraham Lincoln took the presidential oath of office on March 4. The next day, the new president received a message from Major Robert Anderson, commander of the troops holding Fort Sumter, the sole remaining Federal facility in Charleston, South Carolina. Major Anderson's refusal to abandon Sumter had precipitated a lengthy siege, and by March, supplies were running low. They could last another six weeks, Anderson told the president.

Lincoln flatly rejected the notion that any state could leave the Union and believed armed conflict was unavoidable. Nevertheless, he wanted Southern guns to fire the opening shot. He announced he would send unarmed ships with troops and supplies to Fort Sumter. South Carolina leaders had already defined that as an act of aggression, and their response to Lincoln was swift.

General P.G.T. Beauregard, commander of the South Carolina militia forces, was ordered to take control of the fort whether peacefully or by use of force. Beauregard's artillery commenced firing at 4:30 a.m. on April 12. Anderson finally surrendered thirty-six hours later.

On April 15, Lincoln called for seventy-five thousand Union volunteers to put down the rebellion.

NORWICH

Thursday, April 18, 1861

Governor Buckingham received a telegram from Secretary of War Simon Cameron assigning Connecticut a quota of one regiment (approximately one thousand soldiers) for ninety-day enlistments. The governor, who was at his home in Norwich, attended a hastily organized meeting to develop a plan for recruiting and equipping soldiers.

Seventy-one-year-old former mayor John Breed was on the platform, surrounded by those of "younger years and lustier strength." Breed told the assembly, "I had not intended to speak a word here to-day, but the time has come when our colors have been assailed, and these boys [those who had volunteered] have got to see to it. I'm an old man, but I've never seen the time when I so wanted to be back again with the boys as during the last two or three days."

Governor Buckingham brought many in the audience to tears with his comments as he read communications from men offering their services and spoke of his pride in the way the "sons of Connecticut" responded to the crisis.

"Connecticut moves slowly," he said in the most widely quoted portion of his remarks, "but the good old State is true and sure when once started."

A seven-man committee was charged with raising the funds necessary to meet the expenses of sending local boys off to war. Within a short time, they devised a subscription paper titled *The Sinews of War*. Signers would be promising a contribution to a fund for the costs of outfitting and enlisting companies of soldiers from Norwich and the vicinity.

Governor Buckingham immediately pledged $1,000, and the response from the gathered townspeople "made the building fairly shake." Textile manufacturer William P. Greene matched the governor's pledge, bringing another round of cheering. Others followed, and each new pledge brought more applause. A steady stream of telegrams and messages arrived with additional pledges of support for the cause. The meeting was an unqualified success. Organizers reported that the day's pledges totaled $20,000—about $4 million in 2013—a remarkable sum to be raised in a single day in a city of fourteen thousand residents.

Saturday, April 20, 1861

Townspeople gathered at Breed Hall on Saturday evening to express the "sense of the city in this awful hour of our country's peril." As he opened the meeting, Mayor James S. Carew noted it "was in no sense a party meeting, but a meeting where every man could act who loved his country, and was willing to aid in its support."

While the men on the assembly floor were planning the town's participation in the war effort, the town's women had already begun active war work. They filled the balconies and offices of Breed Hall, sewing uniforms for Captain Frank Chester's company, which would be marching off almost immediately.

There may have been band music playing, but this was a deadly serious endeavor. The audience knew that this meeting would decide whether Norwich would support the war. They would also be deciding their role in the war effort. Consequently, every speaker had the audience's close attention.

Attorney George Pratt began by saying the sight of the women at work and such a large group of "earnest men" brought home the painful realities of the situation. The Southern states had rushed madly into war, he said, but they had mistaken the men of the North, and would find them "a wall of fire."

Many of those in attendance had not voted for Abraham Lincoln in November, yet they expressed support for a war precipitated by Lincoln's election. Among them was James Hovey, who noted he'd always been a Democrat, but he "loved his country more than party ties. Jeff Davis has declared that he made war upon none but Black Republicans, but he would find that they were not the only men he had to meet. The North is now united in the support of the constitutional authorities of the government, and would sustain them at all hazards, and at any cost of blood or treasure."

Senator Foster told the audience that party platforms didn't matter much when the country was in danger. "All must now unite in defense of the government and flag," he told them.

John T. Wait, an attorney who would become a congressman after the war, was among those who hadn't voted for the president. Wait told the meeting it was now his duty as an American citizen to give the president his "cordial and unequivocal support in the struggle he is making to preserve the government."

Fear that Washington, D.C., would be taken by the Rebel forces was on the minds of many citizens. Edmund Perkins declared that if the capital fell, he was ready to start at once for Washington. He would assign his property to his family and his creditors, as he was ready to offer his life, which belonged to his country. If Washington were taken, added Ebenezer Learned, "it must be retaken if it costs oceans of blood, and millions of money," which drew hearty cheering and agreement from the assembly.

Norwich's Democratic newspaper, the *Aurora*, editorialized:

> *The war is one of the necessary results of the attempt to break up the Union, and so long as it lasts, we believe it to be our duty, as it is the duty of every man who acknowledges allegiance to the Union under which we live, to sustain the constitutional authorities of the Government, in the exercise of all the powers that may be necessary to bring it to a speedy termination.*

Sunday, April 21, 1861

Reminders that the country was now at war were everywhere. The *Norwich Bulletin* called April 21

> *such a Sunday as the good town of Norwich had never seen before.*
>
> *The beating of drums, the marching and drilling of military companies, the display of flags, and fluttering of bunting, the presence of unusual crowds in the streets, the hum of labor where the uniforms of volunteers were being made, the earnestness and enthusiasm that seemed to animate the multitude, and the eagerness of the people to learn the latest intelligence by telegraph, all combined to make such a Sabbath as will long be remembered.*

Miss Caulkins wrote of the Union flag waving throughout the city:

> *It was swung across Main Street between Apollo Hall and the Wauregan* [Hotel]*; it was displayed from the tower of the First Congregational Church; it fluttered among the groves of Washington Street, rose high over Broadway and the Free Academy, and graced the rope-walk, the engine halls, the numerous factories, the schoolhouses, and several private residences. It was elevated at Greeneville, at the Falls, on the old Court-house, at the Town plot and at Yanticville…The highest of these standards was that which surmounted the Uncas engine house at the Falls—182 feet.*

Captain Frank Chester wasted no time. Sunday or not, his Buckingham Rifles spent much of the day drilling and practicing military maneuvers.

A group of 350 women broke the Sabbath to spend the day at Breed Hall with needles flashing as they continued to sew uniforms for the soldiers in Chester's company. Clergymen in all of the churches preached sermons "appropriate to the times" and led fervent petitions for the Lord's blessing on the departing troops and the nation.

Monday, April 22, 1861

Captain Chester and his men gathered at Uncas Hall before marching to the Norwich train depot. The governor was present to see them off and "marched 'arm-in-arm' with Chester through a large crowd of well-wishers, some cheering, some teary-eyed, all acutely conscious of the new gravity overshadowing their lives."

Meanwhile, Henry Peale was organizing what would become Company C. Both companies were mustered into the Second Connecticut Regiment at New Haven, whose lieutenant was Colonel David Young, the first Norwich man to volunteer his services to the governor. Most of the leadership of the regiment devolved to Young, as commanding officer Colonel Alfred H. Terry was ill much of the time.

The Third Connecticut Volunteer Regiment at Camp Douglas in 1861, taken by Matthew Brady. *Courtesy of the Library of Congress. LC-DIG-ppmsca-34586.*

Enlistment of volunteers continued throughout the city. Edward Harland organized a company called the Norwich City Rifles, whose ranks were promptly filled. They left for the training camp in Hartford on April 29 and were incorporated into the Third Connecticut Infantry Regiment. As they had for Chester's and Peale's men, the citizens of Norwich gave them a hearty sendoff filled with the strange mixture of excitement and sentiment that seemed to go with the occasion. By late May, all three Connecticut regiments had completed their training and were on their way to war.

4

Mr. Aiken and Colonel Perkins Go to Washington

As Norwich rallied to support the president and the newly minted soldiers, Governor Buckingham was taking steps to assure President Lincoln of Connecticut's assistance and support. Communication with Washington, D.C., was cut off when Rebel troops cut telegraph wires and tore up railroad tracks around the city. Any journey to the capital would be hazardous, since it would involve travel through hostile territory. Although the state of Maryland remained in the Union, most of its citizens were blatantly Southern sympathizers. On April 19, the Sixth Massachusetts was attacked in Baltimore as soldiers marched from one train station to another (at the time, there was no direct connection between trains on two different lines).

Governor Buckingham sent two special envoys to deliver dispatches to the president.

William Appleton Aiken

William A. Aiken left Norwich at 6:00 a.m. on April 22, four days after his twenty-eighth birthday. When he reached Philadelphia, he found the city "extremely stirred up and all regular communication with Washington suspended." He met another man who wanted to reach Washington, and the pair spent most of the night trying to find a way to get to the capital.

General William A. Aiken, circa 1894.
Author's collection.

Early the next morning, they secured passage on a special train that was transporting a Pennsylvania regiment to Perryville. Progress was slow, lest the train hit torn-up track and derail.

Since the ferryboats had been taken to Annapolis, Aiken and his companion resorted to hiring a small rowboat to take them across the river. When they landed at Havre de Grace, Maryland, not only did they hear reports of "railroads and telegraphs broken up but there were plenty of men watching to see how many 'd—d Yankees,' as they called them, were going towards Washington."

They were able to get a covered wagon to take them to Baltimore, and when they arrived about 9:30 p.m., they found the streets well lit and filled with people, both soldiers and civilians. Most were wearing badges that proclaimed their sympathy with the Rebels, and "even the few words which the travelers heard as they passed along the crowded halls of their hotel, apprized them that no man could avow Unionism there, and preserve his life in safety for a moment."

Sensibly, they spent the night in their rooms. With the assistance of the hotel owner—a personal friend of Aiken's companion and also of Rebel leaders in the city—they were able to obtain passes that would allow them to continue their journey. For fifty dollars, they got a carriage that took them to Washington, where they arrived about 10:00 p.m. on Wednesday.

Aiken remarked on the sharp contrast between the empty streets and silence he found in Washington and the "hot-blooded" crowd he had heard in Baltimore. When people at the hotel crowded around him with questions about the North, the realization dawned that Washington had truly been cut off from the rest of the country.

Aiken went to the headquarters of Winfield Scott, general in chief of the Union army. The seventy-four-year-old general read Governor

Buckingham's letter and became agitated. He said, "Sir, you are the first man I have seen with a written dispatch for three days. I have sent men out every day, to bring intelligence of the Northern troops. Not one of them has returned. Where are the troops?"

"The number and rapidity of the questions and his very excited manner, gave me a further realization of the critical nature of the situation," Aiken wrote. Aiken also met with Secretary of War Simon Cameron, whose reaction to Governor Buckingham's dispatches was much the same as General Scott's.

Meanwhile, a friend in Washington "advised very strongly against a return by the same route, as my arrival was known and the general nature of my business suspected by Rebel spies, with which the city abounded, and in some quarters least suspected. How the knowledge of my affairs could have been gained has always been a mystery, for I had realized, since leaving Philadelphia, that my personal safety depended entirely upon secrecy and prudence."

Before he left, Aiken went to the White House, where he met President Lincoln. For once, the anteroom was empty of office-seekers and other hangers-on.

> *Mr. Lincoln was alone, seated in his business room upstairs, looking towards Arlington Heights, through a widely opened window. Against the casement stood a very long spy-glass, which he obviously had been using. I gave him all the information I could from what I had seen and heard during my journey. He seemed depressed beyond measure as he asked, slowly and with great emphasis, "What is the North about? Do they know our condition?" I said, no, they certainly did not when I left. This was true enough. He spoke of the non-arrival of the troops under Gen. Butler, and of having had no intelligence from them for two or three days.*

The reality of the separation of South from North was brought home to Aiken as he began planning his return journey to Connecticut. He had money in his pockets, but notes from a New York bank had no value whatsoever in Washington. During his interview with the president, Aiken said, "I had not a cent, although my pockets were full."

The president "instantly perceived my meaning, and kindly put me in possession of such an amount of specie as I desired." The sum was later repaid, Aiken noted.

Aiken's return to Connecticut involved traveling the back roads by "private conveyance" until north of the Pennsylvania line, where he could board a train. At Hanover, he finally was able to telegraph a report to Governor Buckingham, after four days without any communication. It was also the first time in four days that Aiken had seen a United States flag, except while he was in Washington.

That summer, Aiken married the governor's daughter, Eliza, and in October, Aiken enlisted as a navy paymaster and saw action at Port Royal, South Carolina. Early in 1862, the governor appointed him quartermaster general of Connecticut.

The Aikens lived at 157 Washington Street, where they reared their six children. After the war, General Aiken became president of the Norwich Nickel and Brass Company and was president of the trustees of Otis Library for more than forty years. He was active in veterans' groups and was the first commander of Sedgwick Post No. 1 of the Grand Army of the Republic (GAR).

COLONEL GEORGE L. PERKINS

Twenty-four hours after Will Aiken left for Washington, Governor Buckingham sent a second set of dispatches to the president. Seventy-two-year-old Colonel George L. Perkins, a veteran of the War of 1812, volunteered to be the governor's second "envoy extraordinary."

Being six feet in height with an imposing presence and possessing a fearless nature made Perkins an excellent candidate for the hazardous task, despite his age. In addition, for thirty years, Colonel Perkins had been treasurer of the Norwich and Worcester Railroad, which would have afforded him a wide-ranging network of contacts among railroad men and others who would be in a position to help him. He had served in the army as district paymaster in 1812 and had been present at the Battle of Stonington.

He had heard reports that secessionists and traitors were "thick as hornets in Maryland." Colonel Perkins later reported that the trip to Philadelphia was uneventful, and he "determined to take the cars [train] to Perryville and from there to Annapolis by boat, accompanied by a Major Ames, quartermaster of Massachusetts troops."

Colonel Perkins obtained from the president of the Philadelphia and Boston Railroad a letter to the commander at Perryville, asking him to

Colonel George L. Perkins.
Author's collection.

transport Perkins and Ames on one of the company's boats with a twenty-five-man military escort. Colonel Perkins acknowledged "some apprehension" among the boat's passengers because of reports that two vessels were patrolling the Chesapeake Bay with orders to attack any boat headed to Annapolis with troops.

After they arrived at Annapolis, Perkins and Ames reported to General Butler, where the wait at the general's headquarters afforded Perkins a chance to observe Butler in his element and gave him a story about the man later known as "Beast" Butler.

A new officer arrived and reported to Butler. It "was very late, so the young soldier ventured to ask, 'Where am I to sleep, General?'"

Butler, "turning upon him a look never pleasant to contemplate replied with considerable emphasis, 'Young man, do you take me to be chambermaid to this military post?'

"This extinguished the young soldier's desire for sleep" and also left the weary Colonel Perkins resigned to remaining awake until it was time to board a midnight train. General Butler arranged to send Perkins and his companion to Washington on a military train with the Seventh New York and a regiment from Rhode Island.

When they arrived in Washington at noon on Friday, April 26, the first task for Colonel Perkins was to see Secretary of War Cameron. Although a number of people were waiting, the colonel's card was immediately sent up to Cameron. Apparently the porter thought because of the colonel's "commanding figure" that he was "some distinguished magnate" who should not be kept waiting.

Colonel Perkins handed over the dispatches from Connecticut and received answers to be delivered to Governor Buckingham. The dispatches contained an offer from Buckingham to raise a second regiment to be sent to Washington. Secretary Cameron demurred at any immediate assignment of troops but noted that once the capital's defense was in place, troops would be needed to protect communications. If the new troops were three-year enlistees, they would be accepted at once, Cameron said.

Colonel Perkins also saw President Lincoln at the White House, where he found government officials on guard duty. The Honorable Cassius M. Clay of Kentucky, newly named ambassador to Russia, delayed his departure to organize the Strangers' Guard, a sort of Home Guard unit that would protect the Washington Navy Yard and the White House. The 121 volunteers were armed with rifles, revolvers and knives with orders to "fire deliberately and fire low and at the proper time use the knife."

By the time Colonel Perkins made his return trip, New York's Sixty-ninth Regiment was guarding the railroad with orders from Butler to "shoot everyone seen meddling with the track, as you would a dog, and tumble his body down the embankment." Perkins also passed a Union battery of four guns bound for Washington.

Perkins concluded his letter to the governor with a paragraph that summed up the hardships and dangers of the trip—everything from the Baltimore street gang known as the Plug Uglies to the dampness of night:

> *I passed through Egypt* [i.e., Maryland] *without being shot, though in perils of robbers, in perils of mine own countrymen, in perils by plug-uglies, in perils in the city, and in perils among false brethern. In weariness and painfulness, in watchings, in hunger and thirst, in fastings often and in the night dampness.*

Colonel Perkins was credited with bringing back to Connecticut the first reliable reports of troop strength and other information that underscored just how perilous was the position of the nation's capital since the firing on Fort Sumter.

His mission completed, Colonel Perkins returned to Norwich and joined his wife, Emily, at their estate on Broadway, across from the mansion recently purchased by John F. Slater. He lived another twenty-seven years, dying at one hundred years and one month of age.

5

1861—First Bull Run

The new soldiers trained in New Haven and then went to Washington, D.C., where they became part of the Army of Northern Virginia under Brigadier General Irvin McDowell.

Norwich's Dan Tyler was promoted to brigadier general commanding the First Division of McDowell's army. They were stationed at Camp Corcoran and assigned to the defense of Washington, D.C., for most of May.

By July 1861, the ninety-day enlistments were running out, and citizens of the North were clamoring for some sort of military action. President Lincoln prevailed on McDowell to attack Confederate troops. The Connecticut troops were ordered to Manassas on July 16. The next day, they moved to Fairfield Court House as part of the occupying force.

First Battle of Bull Run/Manassas

The three Connecticut regiments and the Second Maine had become the First Brigade of the First Division, commanded by Colonel Erasmus D. Keyes. On July 16, they led the advance to Manassas, with the First and Second Connecticut regiments as the skirmishers in front.

Captain William G. Ely of Norwich was Keyes's adjutant and was mentioned in official reports as having spent twenty-seven hours in the saddle during the battle.

The Rebels withdrew across Bull Run River, and McDowell envisioned an attack along the Rebel right flank. He changed his mind after actually seeing the terrain and spent the next two days reworking his battle plan, apparently not realizing the delay allowed time for Confederate reinforcements to arrive.

General Daniel P. Tyler. *Courtesy of the Faith Trumbull Chapter of the Daughters of the American Revolution.*

Meanwhile, McDowell ordered General Tyler to move some troops ahead to make the Rebels think the army was going straight to Manassas but cautioned Tyler not to engage in any fighting.

Despite his orders, when Tyler saw Confederate troops across the river, they exchanged fire. He took his troops to Blackburn's Ford, where they were surprised by a barrage of fire from Rebel infantry commanded by Brigadier General James Longstreet, which forced Tyler to beat a hasty retreat.

Southern sympathizers played this for all it was worth, claiming victory. Union sentiment was divided between those who saw defeat and others who claimed a great victory that would allow Federal troops to control the Rebel capital at Richmond, Virginia, within two days with just a little more fighting. McDowell planned to quickly defeat the Rebels and bring a prompt end to the war.

That was enough to persuade a large number of civilians—perhaps as many as five hundred—to venture out from Washington to watch what would be humiliation of the Rebels. They anticipated being able to cheer the Union troops as they moved "Forward to Richmond," as the newspaper headlines put it.

McDowell's initial attack on the left flank drove the Confederate forces back to Henry House Hill, where then-colonel Thomas P. Jackson earned the nickname "Stonewall" as Brigadier Geneneral Barnard

Elliott Bee is said to have urged his troops forward, shouting, "There is Jackson, standing like a stone wall." McDowell did not anticipate a strong counterattack by the Rebels, and disorganization was rampant as Union troops were unable to execute his complicated battle plan. Arrival of the Confederate reinforcements sent the Federals into a hasty retreat, widely described as a rout.

After the battle was over, the Connecticut troops returned to Fort Corcoran and then were ordered back to their home state. By the end of July, they were at the end of their enlistment.

On August 10, the men of the Second Regiment returned to Norwich, where they were welcomed with honors and a reception at Breed Hall. Four days later, Captain Harland and his men from the Third Regiment were welcomed in similar fashion.

Absent from the rolls were Norwich boys Joseph Stokes, a private in Captain Chester's company, who died on July 25, and David C. Case of Captain Harland's company, who was killed on July 21. Among the missing were Sergeant Austin G. Monroe, Corporal John B. Jennings and Private James F. Wilkinson of Captain Chester's company and Private Charles A. Murray of Captain Peale's company, all of whom were taken prisoner. Nothing was known of the fate of Private David Rosenblatt of Captain Chester's company, who was recorded as "never heard from."

VIEWING THE BATTLE

Among spectators at the battle site were Senator Foster and Lyme native Alfred Ely, a congressman from New York's Twenty-ninth District, who drove out to Bull Run in a rented carriage with three other men. Ely wrote an account of the day's events in his journal.

They left Washington around 5:00 a.m. Since Ely had obtained a pass to visit the troops from General Winfield Scott, their trip to Virginia was unremarkable. After their noontime arrival at Fairfax Courthouse, they spent a short time viewing the Federal troops who had converged on the village and inspected the courthouse, and then they drove the four miles to Centreville. There they stood on a rise and found they could see the hills in the distance, but not the troops that had already begun fighting, which were obscured by thick woods.

They were not alone. Members of the House and Senate, journalists and other civilian spectators had also come out to view what they expected

Congressman Alfred Ely. *Courtesy of the Library of Congress. Brady-Handy Collection. LC-DIG-cwpbh-03528.*

to be a decisive Union victory that would send the army "Forward to Richmond"—the slogan of the day.

Foster and Ely went to the headquarters of Colonel Dixon S. Miles, commanding officer of the Federal reserve forces, and found him lying on the floor talking with several men. Miles's greeting was cordial enough, Ely said, but the conversation was "desultory" and left him with the impression that Miles was "under the influence of unnatural stimulants."

After leaving, they resumed their drive toward Bull Run, but at a crossing, their carriage was damaged when struck by an army wagon. Foster left the carriage, while Ely looked for a blacksmith to make the necessary repairs.

Senator Foster walked on alone until he came to the Warrenton Turnpike, where a house was being used as a field hospital for one of the Connecticut regiments. The senator found a regimental surgeon "overburdened and without adequate assistance" and promptly volunteered to help care for the wounded soldiers.

After several hours, the surgeon urged Foster to leave because a Rebel cavalry charge placed him in serious danger since he was a civilian and had no protection. Although reluctant to leave, the senator "beat a hasty retreat for several miles and fortunately succeeded in evading the enemy and reaching the Federal lines," according to the *Memorial* biography published after Foster's death.

An editor's note in Ely's journal makes Foster's situation considerably more dramatic. According to Ely, Foster was chased by Rebel cavalry part of the way to Centreville. He escaped and returned to Washington that night in the carriage of U.S. quartermaster general Montgomery Meigs, arriving in time to be in his seat in the Senate chamber on Monday morning, apparently causing something of a stir, as reports had placed Foster among those killed during the battle.

Congressman Ely was not so fortunate. While waiting for the wagon repairs, he encountered some acquaintances from Rochester. They drove a little farther toward Bull Run, hoping to see the Thirteenth New York Regiment, which they'd heard was nearby. Ely and one of the others moved down the road to be closer to the site of the battle.

"When we had gone some seventy-five rods, he declined to go farther and, from fear or prudential motives, turned back and left me alone," Ely wrote.

Ely ended up near the Stone Bridge. Nearby, a reporter asked passersby where he could find General McDowell's headquarters, but no one knew. He repeated the inquiry until he had a response, but the reply left everyone incredulous when the soldier said the battle was lost and the Federal troops were retreating.

Ely soon discovered he was in some physical danger, as a rifle ball struck the dirt in the road near him, and as he and others took shelter behind

A rendering of the retreat at Bull Run by artist Thure de Thulstrup. *Courtesy of the Library of Congress. LC-DIG-pga-00335.*

a large tree, "a cannon-ball or shell came crashing through its branches, scattering the leaves, and adding much to my alarm."

A short time later, an officer on horseback led a company of soldiers out of the woods. He demanded to know Ely's name and whether he was connected with the government. When Ely said he was a representative in Congress, a captain grabbed his arm, and he was taken prisoner.

Although the captain assured him he would not be harmed, Ely found himself quite fearful when brought to Colonel E.B.C. Cash, who drew his pistol "and pointing it directly at [his] head, said, 'G—d d—n your white-livered soul! I'll blow your brains out on the spot.'"

The captain and another officer prevented Cash from carrying out his threat, and the captain explained that Cash was very much excited and had been drinking.

Ely was taken with about six hundred other prisoners to the Libby Prison in Richmond. He kept a diary both to pass the time and record his experiences.

A week after being captured, Ely wrote:

> *July 28.—This is Sunday, and one week has elapsed since the day of my arrest. I am forcibly reminded at this time of an admonition so frequently given to me in the past, by my wife, that work or amusement indulged in upon the Sabbath, must, sooner or later, result in disaster.*
>
> *The full force of this warning, oftentimes and affectionately repeated to me, I now feel with crushing weight. My visit to Centreville was made on Sunday. An all-wise Providence punishes me for a violation of His commandment—a sequence as direct as it is just.*

Congressman Ely remained at Libby Prison six months. On Christmas Day, he was exchanged for Charles J. Faulkner, a Southerner who had been the U.S. ambassador to France. Faulkner had been imprisoned for "disloyal conduct" while in Washington.

6

1862—Antietam

After the battle of Bull Run, most of the men who had enlisted at the beginning of the war had been mustered out at the end of their enlistments. Connecticut's Sixth, Seventh, Eighth and Ninth Regiments were formed as part of Connecticut's quota under the president's second call for troops, in the summer of 1861.

Joining the Sixth was a company of men recruited mainly from Windham County by Captain William G. Ely of Norwich. The Seventh had a company under Captain John B. Dennis of Norwich, who had spent the first months of the war with a Massachusetts regiment. The Eighth Regiment was heavily populated with Norwich men.

The Eighth Connecticut Volunteer Infantry

The Eighth Connecticut Volunteer Infantry mustered at Hartford in September 1861. The men completed their training at Camp Buckingham and left on October 17 for their first stop at Jamaica, Long Island. There, they were the first soldiers to be served by New York's Sons of Connecticut aid group, which presented them with a regimental flag. The officers included Colonel Edward Harland, Adjutant Charles M. Coit and Assistant Surgeon DeWitt C. Lathrop, all of whom were from Norwich.

In Company D, Norwich men filled most of the roster spots, with John E. Ward as their captain; James R. Moore and Charles A. Breed as lieutenants;

and John McCall, Charles Shepard, Amos L. Keables and Joseph E. Fletcher as the sergeants.

In January 1862, the Eighth Connecticut was with Burnside's Expedition in North Carolina. They fought at New Bern, then other locations in Virginia until September 3, when they arrived in Washington, D.C., and bivouacked on the grounds of the Capitol for about a week.

While in the capital, the Eighth and Eleventh Regiments—at that moment, they were the entirety of the brigade Colonel Harland now commanded—marched through Washington and made an excellent impression on the city's residents. They looked so good that a local newspaper identified them as a regiment of the regular army (rather than volunteers), apparently because they marched "in splendid order."

As they waited for the Fourth Rhode Island to arrive at camp, the men of the Eighth Connecticut learned that General George McClellan had been reorganizing the Army of the Potomac. Harland's brigade was assigned to the Third Division of the Ninth Corps. General Isaac P. Rodman was the division commander under General Ambrose P. Burnside.

On September 8, the brigade was ordered to Virginia to join McClellan's army, and by September 16, the soldiers were near Antietam Creek on the Union left line. The Rebel guns on high ground across the creek lobbed the occasional shell toward the Federal troops.

There wasn't much to eat, so the men foraged in the nearby fields for corn to roast and made a meal of the corn and some green fruit they found. Rails and boards of nearby farm fences became their firewood.

Nineteen-year-old Lieutenant Marvin Wait of Norwich was among the soldiers waiting for the battle to begin in earnest on the morning of September 17. Shortly after 7:00 a.m., a shot landed near the Eighth Connecticut, killing three men and wounding four. Some of the soldiers began to retreat, but Lieutenant Wait, covered with dirt and blood from the blast, stood and coolly ordered them back to their positions.

Over the next twelve hours, Union forces made three major assaults on the Rebel positions, but Lee moved his troops around to counter the attacks, and the Federal forces couldn't put enough manpower in any given place to overpower the Rebels and break through their lines. The major attacks were punctuated by smaller skirmishes and clashes along the mile-and-a-half length of the battlefield in the cornfield, the East and West Roads and Sunken Road (also known as Bloody Lane).

Colonel Harland spent the morning trying to find a position where his men would have some protection from Confederate artillery fire. Meanwhile,

A rendering of the Battle of Antietam by artist Thure de Thulstrup. *Courtesy of the Library of Congress. LC-DIG-pga-04031.*

Burnside had been ordered to assault the Georgia troops on the other side of the Rohrbach Bridge (now known as Burnside Bridge). The Eleventh Connecticut was sent forward as skirmishers, but they were mowed down as they attempted to wade across the creek; the regimental commander fell as he led the assault across the bridge itself. Eventually, the Georgia troops ran low on ammunition and retreated. The Union troops captured the bridge and moved south to wade across the creek.

The brigade headed for the series of ridges that climbed to Harper's Ferry Road toward Sharpsburg. Harland gave the order to advance, but only the Eighth Connecticut moved forward. The Sixteenth Connecticut had been moved to support a battery even farther to the left. The men were lying in a cornfield in an apparent attempt to avoid being hit by the Rebel artillery fire.

Whether the officers of the Sixteenth misunderstood or did not hear the order scarcely mattered, but their failure to advance left the Eighth Connecticut alone out in front with no support. Rather than pull the Eighth Connecticut back to wait for the Sixteenth and the Fourth, General Rodman sent the regiment forward and ordered the men to begin firing. He would personally check on the brigades in the cornfield and get them moving, he told Colonel Harland.

Meanwhile, A.P. Hill was quietly moving his men in to reinforce the Confederate troops on the left flank of the Eighth Connecticut, directly toward the Sixteenth. The Sixteenth was somewhat obscured among the high stalks of corn, but so were Hill's soldiers. The men of the Sixteenth had been in the army for barely a month; they had little training in marching and drill and none in using their weapons. There was considerable consternation when they found themselves facing a battery of Rebel cannon directly in front of their position.

Edward Harland. *Courtesy of the Faith Trumbull Chapter of the Daughters of the American Revolution.*

General Rodman frantically tried to get the Sixteenth to swing left to face Hill's troops, a difficult maneuver in good circumstances but nearly impossible for green troops being fired upon. Then Rebels moved to take advantage of the confusion caused by the cornstalks and panicked men hastening to the rear.

As Harland, who was on horseback, perceived the danger and turned toward the Sixteenth, his horse was shot out from underneath him, leaving him to reach the regiment on foot.

Lieutenant Marvin Wait. *Courtesy of the Faith Trumbull Chapter of the Daughters of the American Revolution.*

Meanwhile, the Eighth Connecticut was taking fire from three sides. Witnesses said Lieutenant Wait was closing the ranks of his men and urging them forward when his right arm was shattered by a bullet, causing him to drop his sword. He refused to go to the rear for treatment and instead took up the sword with his left hand and continued urging his men on. After he was hit in the left arm, the leg and in the abdomen, he was helped off the battlefield to the shelter of a fence at the rear. There, a stray bullet hit him, causing the mortal wound. With his final words, Wait asked Private Lewis King, "Are we whipping them?"

The regiment desperately needed direction, but no orders were forthcoming from General Rodman, who had been shot in the chest. Soldiers from the Eighth had taken him to the rear for treatment.

The men of the Sixteenth—panic-stricken by the flying bullets and cannon shot, the noise of the battle and general confusion created by their location in a cornfield—broke ranks and followed another unit to the rear.

Meanwhile, the men of the Eighth continued to advance until they were less than seventy-five yards from the Rebels, who were ordered to fire canister directly into the Connecticut ranks. The Eighth continued forward, sending a steady barrage of fire at their Confederate foes.

Morris and Crofutt wrote a gripping account of the Eighth 's fight:

> *Colonel* [Hiram] *Appelman* [he had been promoted to regimental commander] *tells the standard-bearer never to leave the colors. He responds firmly. One of the color-guard falls; two; three; four; the last, and the standard goes to the ground with him. Private Charles H. Walker* [of Norwich] *springs forward, and seizes it amid the storm of death; strikes the staff firmly in the ground; and shakes out the flag defiantly towards the advancing foe.*
>
> *No re-inforcements come. Twenty men are falling every minute. Col. Appelman is borne to the rear. John McCall falls bleeding.* [Lieutenant Jacob] *Eaton totters, wounded, down the hill.* [Lieutenant Marvin] *Wait, bullet-riddled, staggers a few rods and sinks.* [Captain Eleazur] *Ripley stands with a shattered arm.* [Lieutenant James] *Russell lies white and still.* [Lieutenant Henry F.] *Morgan and* [Lieutenant Edwin G.] *Maine have fallen.* [Whiting] *Wilcox is dead. Men grow frantic. The wounded prop themselves behind the rude stone fence, and hurl leaden vengeance at the foe. Even the chaplain snatches the rifle and cartridge-box of a dead man, and fights for his life.*
>
> *"We must fall back," says Major John E. Ward, now in command. Some protest against what they feel is inevitable; and the hundred men still unscathed are faced to the rear, and marched back in unbroken and still formidable column down the hill. No regiment of the* 9th *Corps has advanced so far, or held out so long, or retired in formation so good.*

Some accounts say it took Major Ward three tries to overcome the determination of the remaining one hundred men to continue the fight.

Retreat was necessary if they were to avoid being flanked by Hill's troops, which would only mean more slaughter. Ward finally persuaded the men to rally around the colors they had defended so valiantly and then retreat.

Harland, as senior ranking colonel, took command of the division and reorganized the regiments into an active defense.

Captain Charles M. Coit. *Courtesy of the Faith Trumbull Chapter of the Daughters of the American Revolution.*

After eight hours of hard fighting, although more than fifteen thousand men were dead or wounded, little had changed. The Federals had moved the Rebel troops back, but their lines held, and the Union troops hadn't broken through. Nevertheless, the fighting continued.

In a letter home, Captain Charles Coit described the battle, proudly confirming the reports that the men stood and fired, then turned and moved back in good order. He noted that although the flags went down, they were lifted again.

The regimental history noted "no other battle took such a toll on the Eighth Connecticut or the regiments of Connecticut as Antietam. Of four hundred men who went into battle, nearly half became casualties. A total of one hundred ninety-four were killed, wounded or missing."

The tallies vary in different accounts, but it appears that 34 men were killed, 149 were wounded and 62 remained missing. The dead included a dozen commissioned officers, nearly half of the unit's leadership.

THE EIGHTH CONNECTICUT AFTER ANTIETAM

From Antietam, the Eighth went on to Fredericksburg, the Siege of Suffolk and various other locations throughout 1863. When the men's enlistments ran out in December, 310 men who had been on the regiment's original rolls reenlisted. A month later, they found themselves on leave at home in Connecticut. When they returned to the front, the regiment became part of the Army of the James and was with Major General Ben Butler in his Bermuda Hundred campaign.

During a single week in May 1864, the regiment lost two more officers, both of who were from Norwich.

Preparing for the siege of Petersburg, the regiment attacked Rebel lines, trying to force them back. The Eighth attacked repeatedly until there was no more ammunition. The men were ordered to fall back and were cheered by the entire brigade as they did so.

For Lieutenant Alfred M. Goddard, who had joined the regiment the previous fall, it was his first and last battle. He was struck by a bullet as he and his men returned to their camp. The wound proved fatal, and Lieutenant Goddard died on May 9, 1864, six weeks short of his twenty-eighth birthday.

In a letter to Goddard's mother, Captain Coit, who had become the commanding officer of the unit, said the entire regiment grieved the loss of a young man who had made such a strong impression despite being in the unit only five months.

On May 16, the Eighth was part of the attack at Drewry's Bluff, or Fort Darling, as the Federals called it. The battle took place in a dense fog that played havoc with communications, which relied heavily on visuals like signal flags. The Eighth held its line for an hour, but in the fog, many of the men became separated from the main unit. A total of sixty men were killed, wounded or taken prisoner.

Among the dead was Captain John McCall. His men were lying prone as they returned Confederate fire, but McCall was sitting upright, and a bullet struck him in the heart. Witnesses said he jumped up and said, "I shall be dead in a minute," and fell backward.

At home in Norwich, the community grieved with the families of the two soldiers. The city's common council passed resolutions formally acknowledging the deaths, attended both funerals and watched as the young men were buried in Yantic Cemetery.

Late in June, the regiment was ordered to the front of the line at Petersburg, and the men of the Eighth spent that entire summer under the hot sun, lying in rifle pits within range of the enemy cannons. What must have been terrible monotony was broken by assaults on the Rebel fortifications. After one charge, in which the Eighth performed especially well, General William F. "Baldy" Smith was heard to remark he "felt like giving a commission to the whole regiment that had done that gallant deed."

For the regiment, the fighting continued—at Cold Harbor, Petersburg and numerous other Virginia locations. Finally, on April 3, 1865, the Eighth was with the Union army advance that went to Richmond.

After a few months of guard and picket duty, the regiment mustered out of service on December 12, 1865, after four years and two months in the army. In that time, the Eighth suffered casualties approximately equal to its original strength. The tattered remains of the regimental colors were placed on display in the Capitol in Hartford.

NORWICH IN THE EIGHTH CONNECTICUT

Edward Harland

Edward Harland—or Ned, as his friends called him—was born in Norwich on June 24, 1832, the second son of Henry and Abigail (Hyde) Harland. He was the grandson of noted watch and clockmaker Thomas Harland. After graduating from Yale College in 1853, Harland returned to Norwich, studied law and passed the bar two years later.

The twenty-nine-year-old lawyer was among the first to volunteer when the war began in 1861. He organized and served as captain of the Norwich Rifles, which became Company D of the Third Connecticut Regiment.

When that ninety-day enlistment ended, Harland began to recruit men to fill the ranks of the Eighth Connecticut. He was colonel and commanding officer of the Eighth until the unit joined Burnside's new Ninth Corps. Harland was then assigned command of the Second Brigade, Third Division—the Eighth, Eleventh and Sixteenth Connecticut Regiments and the Fourth Rhode Island.

Harland successfully led his division during the final assault at Antietam, where he had been assigned to replace General Rodman as commander and was promoted to brigadier general at the end of November.

He returned to command the brigade at Fredericksburg in December and was credited with saving many lives during an assault on Marye's Heights because he held his brigade back in the face of friendly-fire incidents involving another regiment.

In 1863, Harland and his brigade were moved to the Seventh Corps in Virginia's Tidewater region, where they fought at the Siege of Suffolk as the Second Brigade, Second Division. From there, Harland was transferred to the Eighth Corps in North Carolina, where he was commander of the Sub-district of Pamlico, and then commanded a brigade at Wyse Fork in March 1865.

General Harland left the army in June 1865 and returned to Norwich, where he resumed his law practice. The general was active in the Grand

Army of the Republic and other veterans' organizations and spent time in Hartford as the state's adjutant general.

The general also was the inventor of a three-hundred-year calendar the size of a calling card. With tongue firmly in cheek, Harland said he would refund the purchase price if the calendar were unsatisfactory after three hundred years of use.

General Harland served in both houses of the Connecticut legislature and was a probate judge for several years. He later became president of the Chelsea Savings Bank. The general never married and, after his mother's death, lived on at 357 North Washington Street.

After his death on March 9, 1915, Harland was buried in Yantic Cemetery in Norwich.

Charles Morgan Coit

Charles Coit was a banker with a promising career, but he resigned his position as secretary treasurer of the Chelsea Bank to join the Eighth Connecticut in September 1861. Coit was named Colonel Harland's adjutant.

The son of Charles and Sarah (Perkins) Coit, young Charles had connections with many of Norwich's influential families. He was a graduate of Yale, and his abilities seemed to be recognized in every endeavor he undertook. The bank trustees thought so highly of Coit that they voted to keep the position for him until after the war.

He rose through the ranks in his regiment, becoming captain of Company B in March 1862, and fought in all of the regiment's major battles. At one point, Captain Coit was the de facto commander of the entire regiment in the absence of any field officers. Coit was assigned duty as assistant adjutant at brigade headquarters but turned down a promotion to major and an assignment to the brigade field staff to stay with his regiment.

He was wounded at Fair Oaks, Virginia, in early 1865. When he recovered, he returned to his regiment for a time before being mustered out in May 1865. Coit was later brevetted a lieutenant colonel.

Colonel Coit returned to Norwich, where he resumed his position as treasurer of the bank and served for a time as Norwich postmaster.

He and his wife, Mary Hilliard Coit, whom he married in 1872, had two children. Colonel Coit drowned in 1878 while rescuing his son during a sailing accident in New London Harbor. He saved the boy but lost his own life in the effort.

Marvin Wait

Lieutenant Marvin Wait was the son of Norwich lawyer John T. Wait and Elizabeth (Harris) Wait. In the fall of 1861, Marvin left his studies at Union College in Schenectady, New York, and came home to persuade his reluctant parents to permit him to enlist.

While the regiment was on Long Island, Wait was assigned to be Colonel Harland's orderly. When they moved to Maryland, he was promoted to lieutenant and sent on detached duty as a signal officer assigned to General Burnside's Ninth Army Corps until July. After a short trip to Norwich accompanying the body of his friend Charles Breed, who died of typhoid fever at Newport News, Wait rejoined the Eighth Regiment in time for the evacuation of Fredericksburg and the march to Antietam.

Marvin Wait was the youngest officer in the regiment and the first commissioned officer from Norwich to be killed in the war.

In a letter to Lieutenant Wait's parents, Major Ward wrote, "No officer could have been more popular, either with the men or with his brother officers. By his soldierly qualities, good spirits and easy manners he had endeared himself to everyone in the least acquainted with him. He died in a good cause and like a brave man."

The regimental history said of Wait: "The story of his heroic fortitude amid the carnage of battle will be preserved upon Connecticut's historic page along with that of Nathan Hale, the youthful martyr spy."

It was said that Wait's mother was never the same after his death; in any case, she died about five years later. His father continued his law practice and remained active in politics and was a presidential elector in 1864. John T. Wait subsequently served in the Connecticut General Assembly before being elected in 1876 to the U.S. House of Representatives, where he served for ten years.

THE FOURTEENTH CONNECTICUT VOLUNTEER INFANTRY

Listen, young heroes! Your country is calling!
Time strikes the hour for the brave and the true;
Now, while the foremost are fighting and falling,
Fill up the ranks that have opened for you!
—Oliver Wendell Holmes

By the spring of 1862, some people believed that the end might be in sight. The War Department halted enlistments on April 3, and shortly afterward, the president issued a proclamation calling for a season of thanksgiving "for the glorious successes of our armies at the front." Considered together, these events suggested victory was at hand, and enlistments dropped off.

When Governor Buckingham learned the War Department would accept another regiment from Connecticut, he authorized the creation of the Fourteenth Connecticut as a statewide unit. Enlistment was slow in the early months, probably because no true soldier really wanted to spend months at a "camp of instruction"—that is, boot camp. Dwight Morris of Bridgeport was named colonel.

A series of Confederate victories led to the inevitable conclusion that the fighting would go on and more soldiers would be needed. On July 1, President Lincoln called for another 300,000 men to serve for three years or the duration of the war.

Governor Buckingham followed two days later with his own appeal, famously urging Connecticut citizens to "Close your manufactories and workshops, turn aside from your farms and your business, leave for a while your families and your homes, and meet face to face the enemies of your liberties! Haste, and you will rescue many noble men, now struggling against superior numbers, and speedily secure the blessings of peace and good government."

In July, Norwich increased the bounty for new enlistees and stepped up recruitment efforts. By late August, the quota was met. The Fourteenth was at full strength, with more than one thousand men on the rolls.

Two companies of the new regiment were heavily populated with Norwich men: Company F had Captain William A. Tubbs, First Lieutenant Morton Hale and Sergeants James R. Nickels (later promoted to captain) and Frederick E. Schalk, in addition to twenty-one enlisted men. In Company K, the Norwich contingent included Lieutenant James B. Coit, Sergeant Major Henry P. Goddard and Lieutenant George C. Ripley, as well as about forty enlisted men.

The regiment left almost immediately, boarding two steamboats at Hartford with a rousing send-off, which was repeated at Middletown. The next morning, the men reached New York City, where the Soldiers' Relief Association treated them to a hearty meal. They crossed the river to New Jersey, where they boarded railroad cars to Baltimore via Harrisburg and York, Pennsylvania.

During the trip, Norwich's Fred Schalk was injured when he fell thirty feet from a trestle. Sergeant Schalk had apparently left the train car and was attempting to reboard when he lost his footing. He was left behind for treatment of a head injury; when recovered, he rejoined the regiment.

The men of the Fourteenth could be excused for any trepidation they might have felt about moving through Baltimore, where a year before, the Sixth Massachusetts had been brutally attacked. They were pleasantly surprised, according to William Hincks of Company A, who wrote, "Call Baltimore a secession place if you will, but we were treated better here than in any other place on our route." Ladies met the Fourteenth with water, bread and melons. At the Soldier's Relief building, run by citizens of Baltimore, they found plentiful food.

They passed in review before General John E. Wool, who commented to Colonel Morris, "A splendid regiment, not one drunken man in the ranks; too good a regiment to be sent anywhere but to the front!"

The regiment traveled the forty miles to Washington in smelly train cars that had been used to transport cattle and hadn't been cleaned out. The Fourteenth was the first regiment to march through Washington after the second call for more troops, and captains and higher-ranking officers were introduced to President Lincoln, General Grant and other officials on the reviewing stand.

When the men of Company B reached the stand, the president's attention was elsewhere, so they began loudly singing "We Are Coming, Father Abraham," a popular song of the moment. The president straightened, "doffed his high silk hat and bowed and bowed until we were by."

From there, the brand-new regiment was ordered to Antietam, where it was in the thick of the fighting and spent thirty-six hours with fire raining down from heavy artillery and sharpshooters in high positions across Antietam Creek. Men from the Fourteenth captured sharpshooters in the spring house on the Roulette Farm and were heavily involved in the fighting at the Sunken Road (Bloody Lane).

For many miles, the Fourteenth Connecticut had been marching with the Irish Brigade, whose members jeered that it would be impossible to see the Fourteenth because of "the dust they would kick up getting away from Bobbie Lee."

The Irishmen changed their minds after Antietam, where they were repulsed by heavy fire at the Sunken Road, and the Fourteenth Connecticut moved in to reinforce them. After that, the Irishmen recognized the men of the Fourteenth as fighters and had confidence that they would hold their part of the line.

Apparently, the army's ranking officers also recognized the Fourteenth as a fighting unit, since, after Antietam, the regiment was "almost constantly in active service."

7

1863—Port Hudson

Unlike the other regiments that went into service in 1861, the Thirteenth Connecticut didn't go directly to the battlefield, perhaps because the regiment mustered on November 25, and historically, armies didn't fight much during the winter months. As it turned out, nearly half of their time in the service had gone past before the men of the Thirteenth saw any serious fighting.

The Thirteenth Connecticut Volunteer Infantry and Henry Birge

When the war began, Colonel Henry Warner Birge was an aide on the staff of Governor Buckingham and spent the early months of the war helping to organize the first regiments from Connecticut. When the Thirteenth was raised, Colonel Birge became the commanding officer.

Other Norwich men on the command staff were Adjutant George W. Whittlesey, Quartermaster Joseph R. Bromley and Second Assistant Surgeon Nathan A. Fisher. Three company commanders were from the Rose City: Captain James J. McCord and Second Lieutenant John C. Abbott of Company F and Captain Alfred Mitchell of Company K. In addition, Lieutenants William P. Miner and Robert Ripley and more than fifty of the privates were also from Norwich, most of them in Captain McCord's Company.

Henry Warner Birge. *Courtesy of the Faith Trumbull Chapter of the Daughters of the American Revolution.*

The first duty assignment for the Thirteenth was New Orleans. The regiment marched into the city on May 15, 1862, the same day that the military governor, General Ben Butler, issued his General Order 28—the one that declared "when any female shall by word, gesture, or movement insult or show contempt for any officer or soldier of the United States she shall be regarded and held liable to be treated as a woman of the town plying her avocation." That is, they would be treated as prostitutes.

It's unknown whether the Thirteenth was subjected to any of the insults, but the precise drills and spit and polish required by Colonel Birge really paid off because the regiment caused "a marked sensation" as it marched into the city. It was said that observers were quite sure that the Thirteenth was "the finest looking regiment that ever entered New Orleans," and it became a great favorite of General Butler.

For Colonel Birge and his troops, the early months of military life were fairly routine, even boring. The wit of Quartermaster Joseph R. Bromley broke the periods of tedium, and his concern for the regiment's needs became legendary.

At one point, the regiment was moved to a camp about five miles outside the city. In his history of the regiment, Colonel H.B. Sprague told this story:

> *The principal difficulty at this time was in getting wood. Our Quartermaster, never long at a loss for expedients, finally proceeded to the depot of the Carrollton Railroad, and commenced loading his teams. The Superintendent* [of the railroad] *is said to have come up, and to have held the following dialogue with Bromley:*
>
> *"What are you going to do with that wood?"*
> *"Cook rations. (Go on with your loading, Corporal.)"*
> *"Who are you?"*
> *"Bromley, Quartermaster of the Thirteenth Connecticut Volunteers. Allow me, sir, in turn to inquire whom I have the distinguished honor to address."*

"I'm superintendent of this railroad."
"All right. (Go on with your loading, Corporal.)"
"The wood belongs to the railroad."
"So I supposed!"
"But I forbid you to take it."
"Put your protest in writing, in red ink. Tie it with a piece of red tape. I'll approve it and forward it. You see we've got to have wood to cook with. Can't eat beans and pork raw. I'd prefer 'em raw, but the men are so unreasonable, they want 'em cooked."
"But that wood's necessary for the use of the railroad."
"It's necessary for the use of the Thirteenth Connecticut."
"I should like to know how a locomotive is going to run without wood."
"I've often wondered how a regiment could be run without wood."
"General Butler orders me to run this railroad."
"Colonel Birge orders me to run the Thirteenth Connecticut."
"Who's Colonel Birge?"
"Who's Colonel Birge? Why the deuce don't you know Colonel Birge? If there's one man above another that everybody knows, it's Colonel Birge."
"Will Colonel Birge pay for the wood?"
"Colonel Birge pay for the wood? Why no! It's a reflection on your sagacity to ask such a question."
"Who will pay for it?"
"The Quartermaster's Department. If there's one thing above another that I admire in the Quartermaster's Department, it's because they'll always pay for wood. Now, my friend of the railroad persuasion, if you'll come and see me, I'll give you receipts, and help you fix up the proper papers to present to the Quartermaster's Department."
"How long will it be before I get paid?"
"It will be some future day—the futurest kind of a day, I'm afraid."
The Superintendent posted off to see Colonel Birge. Bromley preceded him however, and cautioned sentinels to admit no citizen without a pass. "Halt!" said the sentry; and the Superintendent gave up the pursuit in despair.

Bromley had a way of meeting the regiment's needs, even when out foraging:

The instructions which Bromley gave to Corporal Strange, a member of his staff, as he termed him, were quite significant. "Strange, we're

> *going on an expedition. I want my staff to be on the lookout for turkeys, geese, pigs, and sheep. Don't be the aggressor in any contest. Stand strictly on the defensive; but if you're attacked by any of these animals, show fight, and don't forget to bring off the enemy's dead."*

The Thirteenth was involved in a couple of minor engagements before it saw serious action at Irish Bend on April 14, 1863. The regiment won accolades for discipline and coolness and for capturing an enemy flag.

Perhaps the Thirteenth's finest moment was at Port Hudson, Louisiana; it was certainly one of the best exhibitions of selfless patriotism of the entire war. Control of the Mississippi River was at stake in the summer of 1863. Both North and South saw the river as a major objective; the Confederates needed control of the river as a major supply route. The Union wanted to block the supply route and divide the Confederacy in half. The Federals already controlled ports at Memphis and New Orleans, but to control the river, the Union would need Vicksburg and Port Hudson along the river's middle section. It would be difficult to secure Port Hudson, as the high bluffs along the riverbanks were an ideal place for cannons and other artillery that would make an assault very difficult.

Union troops mounted a siege of Port Hudson. General Ulysses Grant was farther upriver at Vicksburg, while General Nathaniel P. Banks, Butler's replacement as commander of the Department of the Gulf, drew the assignment at Port Hudson. Banks had about 30,000 troops available. He hoped to storm the fort, overwhelm the 7,500 Confederate troops and end the siege quickly; he could then send his men to assist Grant at Vicksburg.

On May 24, the Thirteenth was supposed to be held in reserve at the rear of the battle, but "by sheer force of enthusiasm and stress of the emergency, it worked its way to the fore-front of the hottest battle," the regimental history bragged.

Repeated unsuccessful assaults on the fort with heavy losses had a frustrated Banks calling for one thousand volunteers who would have special training to form a "storming column" that would launch one final, desperate attempt to take the fort—a "forlorn hope."

Colonel Birge volunteered to lead the assault team but didn't tell his men, hoping to avoid undue influence on whether they themselves would volunteer. Nevertheless, they found out, and 241 men from the Thirteenth volunteered for the Forlorn Hope mission.

They knew exactly what they were getting into and recognized that the odds of returning were low. The regimental history describes the men's preparation for the assault:

> *Some of the officers wrote out their wills, transferred money and keep-sakes to comrades who were to remain behind and wrote their last messages to loved ones at home...They knew well the ground over which they would have to pass, and that the chances were against their ever returning. It was a volunteer service, in a trying hour, and at the risk of life itself.*

The rest of the regiment told the colonel that they wanted to be the first supporting unit right behind the Forlorn Hope group. They, too, knew what they were volunteering for—that they were effectively joining the "Forlorn Hope" assault group. Fortunately for all concerned, the Rebels surrendered before the Forlorn Hope assault was ordered forward.

The regimental history correctly called Forlorn Hope one of the most heroic incidents of the war, an "imperishable memorial of the self-sacrifice and courage of the men, and their leader, both of whom the country had every reason to feel proud."

The storming column was given the honor of receiving the surrender with Lieutenant Colonel Joseph Selden of Norwich and his Twenty-sixth Regiment right behind them. In addition, the Thirteenth's band, considered the best in the Gulf Department, and the regiment's colors were chosen for the formal surrender ceremony.

After a veteran furlough, the men of the Thirteenth returned to duty in time for the Shenandoah campaign and went from there to Winchester, where Birge, by then a general, commanded a division.

NORWICH IN THE THIRTEENTH

Henry Warner Birge

Henry Warner Birge was born on August 25, 1825, the son of Backus Warner Birge and Lucy (Coit) Ripley. Both came from illustrious families, and his mother could trace her ancestors back to William Bradford, of Mayflower fame. His mother's sister, Eliza, was married to Governor Buckingham. Birge married Eliza Walbridge Meech, who came from a wealthy Norwich family. They had three children.

Birge held the rank of major and was commanding officer of the Fourth Connecticut Volunteers, a three-year unit (later to become the First Connecticut Heavy Artillery). Later that year, he was promoted to colonel and given command of the Thirteenth Connecticut.

By 1864, Brigadier General Birge was brigade commander in the second Red River campaign and then commander of the troops at Baton Rouge, Louisiana. From there, he went to Shenandoah Valley as a division commander with General Sheridan, who recommended that Birge be brevetted major general of volunteers for gallantry at the Battle of Cedar Creek. General Birge was in Atlanta, Georgia, when the war ended.

General Birge stayed in the army until October 1865, when he resigned and returned to Norwich. Five years later, he returned to Georgia, where he and his family lived in Camden. The 1870 census showed Birge's occupation as "saw miller."

General Birge died on June 1, 1888, in New York City and is buried in Yantic Cemetery in Norwich.

Joseph R. Bromley

Joe Bromley was a Norwich merchant when he enlisted as quartermaster of the Thirteenth Regiment. Ill health forced his resignation from the regiment in December 1863.

He stayed in Louisiana and served as a member of the Constitutional Convention that was convened to reestablish Louisiana as a free state. Although he was nominated to represent his district in the U.S. Congress, he declined.

Bromley was the collector of internal revenue in Thibidoux, Louisiana. Bromley and his wife, Vesta Iantha Stevens, had a son, who died at age twelve, and a daughter.

Bromley died in New Orleans on September 3, 1866, and was "buried at sea when the remains were sent North," according to a family genealogy. His wife survived him by nearly forty years.

The Twenty-sixth Connecticut

On August 27, 1862, Norwich residents filled Breed Hall for yet another war meeting and again voted to increase the enlistment bounty offered by the town, this time to $100. Three nights later, a town meeting ratified the war meeting's action and then moved to the question of seeking volunteers. From the floor came offers of incentives for new recruits and money for the support of their families.

Together with an evening rally, the meeting secured enough enlistments, largely from New London County, to fill the ranks of a new regiment, the Twenty-sixth Connecticut, which mustered at Norwich.

The regimental officers included Joseph Selden as lieutenant colonel, Stephen B. Meech as adjutant, Benjamin F. Tracy as quartermaster and Elisha Phinney as assistant surgeon. In Company B, Captain Clarke Harrington and Second Lieutenant James S. Maples were from Norwich; in Company D, it was Captain Samuel T. Huntoon and First Lieutenant Timothy W. Tracy. Company F had Captain Loren A. Gallup, First Lieutenant Edward W. Eels and Second Lieutenant Hervey F. Jacobs, all from Norwich. In Company G, Captain John L. Stanton and Second Lieutenant Pliny Brewer were from Norwich. Also from Norwich were 125 of the regiment's privates.

On November 14, the regiment marched through Norwich on its way to New York and then headed to its first assignment in New Orleans. After time on guard duty and drill, the regiment was ordered north for the assault on Port Hudson as part of General Neal Dow's brigade.

During the first assault on May 27, the regiment was on the extreme left, where the men were exposed to heavy enemy fire. Colonel Kingsley was wounded, and Lieutenant Colonel Selden assumed command. Captain John Stanton died instantly when he was struck by a bullet as he led the attack, urging his men to follow him.

By their courage and gallantry as well as coolness under fire, the men of the Twenty-sixth convinced observers that nine months' men could hold their own in battle. The Twenty-sixth, commanded by Lieutenant Colonel Selden, led the June 14 assault on Port Hudson. The men reached a ravine about three hundred yards from the Rebel fortifications and held their own against the heavy fire, which pinned them down until darkness concealed their withdrawal from the field. The regiment received a special commendation for its courageous and veteran-like behavior.

At Port Hudson, Lieutenant Colonel Selden reported that the Twenty-sixth had 26 men killed and 151 wounded. Most of the casualties were sustained on May 27 in a charge "through a storm of grape and canister from the rebel batteries."

Sergeant Albert Smith of Salem was at the rear of the retreat and turned to fire again when he was hit. Passing Captain Loren Gallup of Norwich as he was being carried to the rear, he shook hands and said, "Goodbye! Tell my friends I hope to meet them in heaven."

Joseph Selden. *Author's collection.*

Gallup himself was saved from being hit when a bullet heading for him instead stuck a rifle directly in front of him, with enough force to break the band. Another soldier felt the impact of a shot, but the bullet actually hit his tobacco box. One soldier was struck in the belt clasp.

The members of the regiment were discharged and joyously

The Port Hudson monument. *Author's collection.*

Left: The crossed rifles detail on the Port Hudson Monument. *Photo by author.*

Below: The inscription on the Port Hudson Monument. *Photo by author.*

welcomed home at the end of their ninety days in the army. Little Plain, the park near St. Patrick's Church, was the scene of a formal ceremony and reception. A banner hung at the entrance welcomed the men home, and another, lettered "Port Hudson," hung on the speakers' platform occupied by the governor, the mayor, members of the common council, Colonel Kingsley and others.

Sixty years later, the town dedicated a monument commemorating the Twenty-sixth Connecticut Infantry and its heavy losses at Port Hudson. In 1899, the general assembly appropriated $1,000 for such a monument, and that amount was matched by the city.

The monument is a twenty-seven-foot-high obelisk with horizontal bands that divide its height into three sections. The lowest section of the front shows crossed rifles with bayonets wrapped in a wreath above a canteen and haversack, symbols of the infantry. Other decorations include a representation of the regimental badge and a haversack with the number twenty-six on it.

The monument was dedicated on August 19, 1902, the day of the regiment's thirty-ninth reunion. Surviving members of the regiment met at the Buckingham Memorial for a business meeting and then moved to Little Plain, where the monument had been erected.

NORWICH IN THE TWENTY-SIXTH INFANTRY

Joseph Selden

At forty, Joseph Selden would have been an old man to his teenage privates. Colonel Selden was born in 1822, making him much older than most of those who enlisted. He would have been well into his career. He was also a married man—he and his wife, Caroline (Lord) Selden, had five children. He traded a large, comfortable house in the city's fashionable Laurel Hill section for the rigors and discomfort of camp life. Perhaps Selden wished to avoid being drafted—he was well within the applicable age range. Or perhaps he had an upsurge of patriotism or was responding to a sense of duty. It is likely he would have found a nine-month commitment more palatable than three years. Whatever the reason, Selden enlisted as lieutenant colonel for the Twenty-sixth Connecticut.

Not long after his service ended, at the request of Governor Buckingham, Selden returned to New Orleans to encourage reenlistment among soldiers stationed there.

After the war, Selden served as internal revenue collector in Norwich from 1869 to 1885 and was a partner in an insurance agency. He died in 1887.

Loren A. Gallup

Loren A. Gallup was just twenty-two when the war began. He enlisted in the Twenty-sixth as captain of Company F. After his service was completed, at the governor's request, he returned to New Orleans with Colonel Selden on the recruiting mission. In August 1863, the governor dispatched Captain Gallup to check on conditions at military hospitals where Connecticut soldiers were being treated.

Captain Gallup married Elizabeth Hooker Kinne in 1864. They had four children. In 1865, he became a partner in L.W. Carroll & Company, wholesalers of paints, oil and wool. He died in 1896 at the age of fifty-eight.

8

1863—Second Winchester

In early summer, the news arrived that a New London County regiment would be formed. On July 28, Governor Buckingham ordered the Eighteenth Connecticut Volunteer Infantry into camp at the Fairgrounds in Norwich, near what is now known as East Great Plains. Later that day, Captain Isaac Hakes and the 110 men of Company E marched into what became known as Camp Aiken. Nineteen days later, more than 1,000 men were on the rolls of the regiment. The Eighteenth Connecticut was the first regiment mustered from the Rose City, and with more than 250 of its men enlisted, the city claimed the regiment as its own and took a special interest in how its troops fared.

The colonel was William G. Ely. At twenty-four, he was a seasoned veteran of both combat and command with the distinction of having fought in both the first land and the first naval engagements of the war.

Ely was with the Sixth Connecticut as it was ordered south for the assault on Port Royal, South Carolina, the first naval engagement of the war. After a five-hour battle, the Union bombardments succeeded in quieting the enemy guns, and Federal troops prepared to land. He had been on the steamboats off Hilton Head, watching as the Union artillery vanquished the Rebels. Ely was the commander of the Connecticut troops sent ashore to secure the victory.

When it became known that a Norwich regiment was being formed, Will Ely lobbied his father, the revenue assessor for Eastern Connecticut, to speak with the governor about giving him command of the new unit. It's unknown whether Jesse Ely intervened, but Governor Buckingham approved Will Ely's promotion to full colonel and his appointment as commanding officer of the Eighteenth Connecticut.

The regimental history lists the officers as follows:

- Colonel: William G. Ely (previously lieutenant colonel of the Sixth Infantry, subsequently brevetted brigadier general)
- Quartermaster: Dwight W. Hakes (afterward captain and brevet major)
- Surgeon: Charles M. Carleton
- Sergeant Major: Joseph P. Rockwell (promoted to adjutant and captain)
- Quartermaster Sergeant: William Carruthers (promoted to first lieutenant)
- Commissary Sergeant: Henry Hovey
- Company C: Captain Isaac H. Bromley
- Company F: Captain Henry Peale (promoted to major and lieutenant colonel)

While the Eighteenth Connecticut was in camp, a steady stream of visitors delivered treats and items of comfort for the soldiers. On August 22, the day of their departure, their final visitor was Governor Buckingham, who brought their regimental colors.

General William G. Ely. *Courtesy of the Faith Trumbull Chapter of the Daughters of the American Revolution.*

Each Connecticut regiment had a color guard that carried the national and regimental flags. In the era before electronic communication, the flags were the locator and rallying point for the soldiers of a unit—they would "follow the colors" into battle. As long as the colors were held up, there was a chance; defeat meant the colors would be surrendered to the enemy.

The ladies of Norwich provided the regimental colors for the Eighteenth Connecticut. The Union flag was made from heavy silk by Tiffany & Company, the New York jeweler, which also made banners. The name of the regiment and the stars were embroidered in silver, and a silver spearhead shone at the tip of the staff. The regimental flag hadn't been finished in time for the departure but was sent to the regiment when it reached Baltimore.

The flags for the Eighteenth Connecticut were among the first Tiffany's created under contract with the state. Researchers at the Connecticut State Archives found that, at the beginning of the war, the unit flags were silk with designs painted on the fabric, but the material tore and frayed in the wind, so Quartermaster General William Aiken decided to seek heavier fabric with embroidered designs. John Almy lobbied for Tiffany's to be the source for the new flags.

Although Almy was the state's assistant quartermaster and working as agent for Connecticut in New York City, he grew up in Norwich. His family lived just up the street from Quartermaster General Aiken on Washington Street.

Almy also had family connections with Tiffany's. His brother's sister-in-law was Lydia Ballou Young, the widow of Tiffany's co-founder John B. Young. After he retired, John and Lydia Young lived in the Ballou family home, next door to the Almys. Charles Lewis Tiffany, the other co-founder, was married to Young's sister, Harriet. Thanks to Almy's connections, Connecticut's cost for the flags was the considerably reduced amount of $100 to $160 apiece ($2,300 to $3,600 in 2013 dollars).

Once Colonel Ely accepted the flag on behalf of the regiment, it was time for the regiment to march into the city. Norwich was used to staging send-offs for individual companies, but this was the first regiment to leave for the war directly from Norwich.

The city was decorated for the occasion in what was described as its "holiday attire," that is, banners and bunting hung everywhere and Union flags waved from downtown buildings as well as boats in the Thames River. Ladies waved handkerchiefs from windows and balconies along the marchers' route.

The regiment first went to assist in the defense of Baltimore and then went to western Virginia before being ordered to occupy Winchester, Virginia, where the men would experience the first battle in the ten months they had been in uniform.

During the Civil War, Winchester was desirable as a transportation center where railroads and main thoroughfares intersected. In an article titled "Winchester During the Civil War," J.M. Berkey suggests that possession of Winchester meant having control of the Shenandoah Valley and its resources. If the Union held Winchester, Lee would have to stretch his troops thin if he were to protect Richmond. Confederate possession of Winchester put Lee within striking distance of Washington and gave him a route for an invasion of Pennsylvania.

Over the four years of the war, possession of Winchester seesawed a dozen or more times. It was considered hard to defend because the terrain kept the defenders from getting adequate intelligence about oncoming enemy troops.

The Second Battle of Winchester began on June 13, 1863, as Confederate forces under Lieutenant General Richard Stoddert Ewell—newly replacing the late Thomas "Stonewall" Jackson as corps commander—mounted repeated attacks on the Union positions. After two days of fighting, Major General Robert Milroy ordered the Federal troops to evacuate Winchester on the night of June 15. Ewell, who had figured out the only remaining route for retreat, positioned his troops to intercept Milroy's troops, and fighting began again.

During the second of two Federal charges, the Eighteenth Connecticut became separated from the brigade, and Ely ordered his men forward yet again. Although the Federal troops charged three times, they were overwhelmed by the Confederate forces and surrendered. Altogether, the Eighteenth Connecticut recorded 597 men killed, wounded and captured. The regimental history counted 31 killed and 44 wounded, including 5 commanders of companies, a testimonial to the fierceness and severity of the fighting. The others were captured.

The Eighteenth Connecticut fought so ferociously that Confederate general James Walker stopped his troops as they cheered their victory by telling them they had been fighting only one regiment, not an entire army. When Colonel Ely presented his sword in surrender, General Walker commented, "You have made us a good deal of trouble this morning."

Observing the damage to the hilt and blade of Ely's sword as he presented it in surrender, General Walker asked when the damage had been done. When Ely replied it had been that morning, the general replied, "You deserve to keep this—here are the marks of bravery and honor. I will give orders that it be returned to you, sir."

Colonel Ely and a large number of his men were taken prisoner and transported to Libby Prison outside Richmond. Ely's sword was, in fact, shipped to Libby and kept in the prison office for the early part of Ely's incarceration; later, it was shipped to his father in Norwich.

In the confusion of gathering the prisoners of war, Major Henry Peale, who was still mounted, was able to slip away with about thirty men. The soldiers of Company D also seized an opportunity to escape and reunited with Peale at Harper's Ferry. In all, about two hundred of the regiment's men were able to elude Rebel capture.

Libby Prison. *Courtesy of the Library of Congress. LC-USZ62-25518.*

Among those who escaped was Color Sergeant George Torrey (of Woodstock), who took the regimental flag—the one presented by the ladies of Norwich—and wrapped it around his waist to avoid having the colors captured. There it stayed for two days.

Months later, in a speech to the regiment, General Milroy told the Eighteenth Connecticut, "You come from a state whose soldiers never disgrace themselves nor their flag. I am proud of you."

Of those captured, most of the privates were paroled, but the officers of the Eighteenth Connecticut were kept at Libby and Belle Island until the following spring. Libby Prison was a warehouse requisitioned for use as a prison. It was overcrowded, but at least the men there had a roof over their heads. Those at Belle Isle were consigned to the outdoors with no shelter from heat or cold.

There were a number of attempts to escape from Libby, the most dramatic of which occurred on February 9, 1864. Colonel Ely was among the 109 officers who used a pocket knife, chisels, part of a hinge and whatever else they could find to dig a tunnel out of the building. It took them nearly three weeks to dig a fifty-three-foot tunnel that emerged in a carriage shed. To escape, the men had to let themselves down the three stories of the chimney and then crawl through the tunnel.

Colonel Henry Peale. *Author's collection.*

About half of those who escaped reached Union lines. Colonel Ely was among the unfortunate forty-eight who were recaptured. Ely was about forty miles away from Libby and within two miles of Union troops when Rebel troops intercepted him. Two officers drowned during their escape attempt. In addition to individual punishment for the escape attempt, the commandant of the prison had the basement filled with enough gunpowder to blow up the entire facility as a deterrent to further escape attempts.

Meanwhile, under the command of Major Henry Peale, the regiment reorganized and joined General French and the Third Army Corps to chase General Robert E. Lee and his Rebel troops. In October, they were rejoined by the paroled soldiers and remained in camp at Martinsburg, Virginia, for the winter.

After a furlough at the end of March, when fighting resumed in the spring of 1864, the Eighteenth Connecticut was ordered to join Siegal's expedition and left Martinsburg on April 29, heading to New Market.

Going into the Battle of New Market on May 15, 1864, the Eighteenth Connecticut had marched fifteen miles in heavy rain. The exhausted men stood knee-deep in mud to lead the extreme advance in a five-hour battle with "unquestioned gallantry." They were badly outnumbered by the enemy and forced to retreat with Rebels nipping at their heels. Peale's report described their conduct as both effective and courageous.

Colonel Ely was finally released from Libby and rejoined the regiment, resuming command in time for the Battle of Piedmont, where they routed the Rebels and captured 2,500 soldiers and five thousand weapons, according to Colonel Ely's report. Yet again, the Eighteenth Connecticut led the advance in the first charge against the enemy. During the battle, 127 men were killed or wounded. Minié balls and cannon shot pockmarked the flags as all but one of the color guard was killed during the battle.

Few of the battles fought by the Eighteenth Connecticut were considered major encounters like Gettysburg or Antietam, but all were critical. The Shenandoah Valley was a backdoor route into Pennsylvania and Maryland, and once or twice a year, Confederate general Jubal Early made the attempt to get past the Union forces.

Invariably, Early's troops outnumbered the Federals left to guard the corridor, so the Eighteenth Connecticut and the other Northern troops always encountered hard fighting.

NORWICH IN THE EIGHTEENTH CONNECTICUT

William Grosvenor Ely

Although Colonel Ely is most closely identified with the Eighteenth Connecticut, when he resigned from the army, he was commander of the Second Brigade, First Division of the Army of Western Virginia. He was brevetted brigadier general a short time later.

Ely trained as a civil engineer at Brown University and worked for Rogers Locomotive Works after graduation. The company had sent him to Cuba, but as soon as the war began, he returned to the United States to enlist. He reached Norwich just in time to enlist in Company A of the First Connecticut on April 22, 1861. Within a week, he had been promoted and commissioned a first lieutenant, and a month later, he was promoted to captain.

After he left the army, General Ely returned to Norwich and married Augusta Greene, whose father, William P. Greene, was among Norwich's major manufacturers. Their house was on what is now the site of Cranston building on the Norwich Free Academy campus. Will Ely became a manufacturer, at first on his own, then joined the family firm and served as treasurer of the Falls and Shetucket companies.

Henry Peale

Henry Peale was part of the Connecticut State Militia before going off to war as part of the Second Connecticut Volunteer Infantry in 1861. He completed his ninety-day obligation just after Bull Run. He served a short period as Norwich fire chief before he joined the Eighteenth Connecticut, where he was captain of Company F.

Peale's management skills and bravery led to his promotion to major about a month before Second Winchester, where Colonel Ely and many of the others were captured. Major Peale was able to slip away with about two hundred men and reform the regiment at Maryland Heights. He continued as commander until Colonel Ely's return.

About the time the unit mustered out in June 1865, Peale was promoted to lieutenant colonel. He returned to Norwich and resumed running the carpenter's shop he had at Central Wharf, not far from his home at the corner of Pearl and Asylum Streets. Peale died in June 1898.

Joseph Tracy

Eighteen-year-old Joseph Tracy joined the Yantic Fire Engine Company in 1861. He was elected clerk treasurer on March 29, 1862, perhaps because of his excellent, clear handwriting.

Just a few months later, on August 7, 1862, Tracy enlisted in the Eighteenth Connecticut, serving as a musician. He was wounded at Snickers Gap, Virginia, on July 18, 1864, and died of the wound at Sandy Hook, Maryland. The fire company's resolution acknowledging his death was drawn up and placed in the fire company records, with a copy given to Tracy's family.

> Minutes of the Yantic Fire Engine Company
> *October 24, 1864*
> *Word has been received of the death of Joseph Tracy, who was wounded in action and died at Sandy Hook, Maryland. Foreman Albert Stafford calls a special meeting of the Fire Company to draw up a Resolution regarding Tracy's death. Foreman Stafford, James Dearden and Samuel Harrison were appointed to a committee to make arrangements for his funeral, including receiving the body, the opening of the grave and obtaining a suitable hearse. The Fire Company voted to attend the funeral wearing the usual badges of mourning.*

9

1863—Gettysburg

Less than a year after their baptism by fire at Antietam, the Fourteenth Connecticut had become the "Brave Fourteenth" and sometimes the "Fighting Fourteenth," a veteran unit with a reputation for reliability and hard fighting.

When it reached Chancellorsville, the Fourteenth Connecticut was again in the thick of the fighting, and the men performed with "great coolness" under fire. Again, the regiment suffered heavy losses; it was said the men "fell like ninepins in an alley before the well-aimed ball of a skillful bowler."

At Fredericksburg, not only was the Fourteenth part of the initial assault, but it was also the only Connecticut regiment in the thick of things. The regiment made three charges before it was ordered to retreat. A severely wounded Lieutenant Colonel Perkins was among the regiment's 122 casualties. In just a year, the Fourteenth Connecticut's strength had dropped from the 1,015 men who left Hartford in 1862 to 219.

As Independence Day 1863 approached, the Fourteenth Connecticut found itself in Pennsylvania. The men had been ordered to leave their camp at Uniontown, Maryland, on July 1 to march toward Gettysburg. That night, the regiment was assigned picket duty along the Baltimore Pike.

The next morning, the Fourteenth Connecticut was sent to the top of Cemetery Ridge in Gettysburg. As the men waited expectantly, a young drummer boy was riding an officer's horse to the rear. The horse became agitated and threw the boy to the ground and then ran toward the regiment, striking Captain James B. Coit in the face and chest. Incredibly, the injury was neither fatal nor disfiguring. Captain Coit missed the battle but rejoined the regiment within a few days.

Late in the afternoon of July 2, the regiment was moved about two hundred yards farther to the left, where the men positioned themselves behind a stone wall near the headquarters of General Alexander Hayes, the division commander. They remained there for the night, with their knapsacks "plumb up to the base of the stone wall and pillowed our heads thereon, not being allowed to divest ourselves of any other arms or equipment," recollected Sergeant E.B. Tyler of Company B. They slept as well as they could, considering the noise surrounding them and contemplation of the day ahead.

On the morning of July 3, men from the Fourteenth Connecticut captured the Bliss farmhouse and barn, storming the buildings in a hail of bullets from the Rebel sharpshooters inside. When ordered, they burned the buildings.

That afternoon, the Fourteenth Connecticut was positioned just north of the "copse of trees" on Cemetery Ridge, directly in front of Confederate general Isaac Trimble's troops, who would be part of the assault later known as Pickett's Charge. The one hundred men who then constituted the regiment were shifted to fill in the space previously occupied by a battery and had to stretch out to avoid leaving a gap, meaning their line was only one man deep.

They watched as fifteen thousand men approached their position, chillingly described in Page's regimental history:

> *All eyes were turned upon the front to catch the first sight of the advancing foe. Slowly it emerged from the woods, and such a column! Eleven brigades of Pickett's Division advancing obliquely upon the Second Division of the Second Corps…There were three lines, and a portion of a fourth line, extending a mile or more. It was, indeed, a scene of unsurpassed grandeur and majesty.*
>
> *It is no wonder that Major Ellis in his official report said, "It was magnificent." As far as the eye could reach could be seen the advancing troops, their gay war flags fluttering in the gentle summer breeze, while their sabers and bayonets flashed and glistened in the midday sun.*
>
> *Step by step they came, the music and rhythm of their tread resounding upon the rock-ribbed earth. Every movement expressed determination and resolute defiance, the line moving forward like a victorious giant, confident of power and victory.*
>
> *If one listened, he might hear the voice of the commander, "Steady men, steady." There is no swaying of the line, no faltering of the step. The*

advance seems as resistless as the incoming tide. It was the last throw of the dice in this supreme moment of the great game of war.

On, on, they come and slowly approach the fence that skirts the Emmettsburg road. Watchful eyes are peering through the loosely built stone wall. Anxious hearts are crouched behind this rude redoubt.

Hardly can the men be restrained from firing, although positive orders had been given that not a gun should be fired until the enemy reached the Emmettsburg road.

It was, indeed, an anxious moment. One you can see is looking at the far off home he will never see again. Another is looking at his little ones, as he mechanically empties his cartridge-box on the ground before him, that he may load more quickly, determined to part with life as dearly as possible. Others are communing with Him before whom so many will shortly have to appear.

Slowly the great line moved forward until it reached the fence. The men mounted to cross when the word fire! fire! ran along the Union line, crack! crack! spoke out the musketry, and the men broke from the fence as if swept by a gigantic sickle swung by some powerful force of nature. Great gaps were formed in the line, the number of slain and wounded could not be estimated by numbers, but must be measured by yards.

Yet on came the second line in full face of the awful carnage. No longer could the measured tread be heard, no longer were the orders of the commanding officers audible for the shrieks of the wounded and groans of the dying filled the air, but on they came, meeting with the same fate as their comrades.

The third line wavered and faltered, even their courage forbidding them to face such a storm of musketry. The color-bearers now advanced, apparently in obedience to previous orders, and, attended by their color-guards, planted their battle flags in the ground near each bearer. Then the firing being too hot for them, lay down, waiting for their men to advance and rally around them. One of them in particular was in advance of the others and planted his flag not more than ten rods distant from and in front of the center of the Fourteenth. The men of the regiment still actively continued firing. Several of the men were fortunate in having two breech-loaders for while one was loading the other was firing. So rapid was this firing that the barrels became so hot that it was almost impossible to use them, some using the precious water in their canteens to pour upon the overworked guns. Accounts seem to agree that the Confederate line broke quicker in the immediate front of the Fourteenth than anywhere else, and seeing this a shout went up from the regiment, which was taken up and echoed and reechoed along the whole Union line.

> *In vain did the Confederate commanders attempt to reform their broken columns, colors were dropped and the men fled in confusion. Major Ellis gave the order to the regiment to fire left oblique to dislodge some of the Confederates who had come uncomfortably near the front of an adjoining battery. The regiment had just turned when a daring and audacious Confederate jumped upon the gun of a battery which had been left about two rods in front, when the battery withdrew for want of horses, and waved his hat in his hand for his comrades to follow. He did not remain there an instant, but fell riddled through. With the help of the regiment's crossfire, the rebels in front of the neighboring battery were soon in full retreat.*

At one point in the battle, Major Ellis noticed a Confederate regimental flag thrust into the ground ten rods (fifty-five yards) in front of the Fourteenth and asked for volunteers to go out and capture it.

Sergeants Hincks and Broatch and Lieutenant Brigham leaped the fence that sheltered the regiment. The Fourteenth Connecticut held its collective breath and watched as Brigham fell and Hincks outpaced Broatch to grab the flag and race back to safety through a hail of bullets.

The flag belonged to the Fourteenth Tennessee and was inscribed with a lengthy list of the unit's previous engagements, which included Fredericksburg, Chancellorsville and Sharpsburg (Antietam). Sergeant Wade said of Company F:

> *By this time the Fourteenth Connecticut were all excited; they remembered Antietam, Fredericksburg, and Chancellorsville, and over the wall they went; nothing could stop them, and soon they were fighting hand-to-hand with the rebels. We captured six battle-flags and forty prisoners; and over one hundred prisoners came in afterwards.*

Later, Sergeant William Hincks was awarded the United States Medal of Honor for his bravery.

The Fourteenth Connecticut numbered about 160 men going into the battle; by its end, there were just 100 left. They fought so fiercely they gave the illusion of a much larger force, much to the amazement of a Confederate colonel who thought his men were fighting an entire army.

By August 18, only about eighty of the regiment's original one thousand men remained. Their greatest trial in that summer of '63 may not have been the fighting; by then, they were used to the routine of tedium punctuated by abject terror. What they were not accustomed to was the new recruits who continued to arrive, staying only a few days before they deserted. Many enlisted under a false name and had to check the name written inside their caps before they could answer at roll call. The veterans found it hard to trust the new men and declared few could be trusted on picket duty—too many had taken the opportunity to desert under cover of darkness.

Fighting near farms had other challenges beyond the obvious. One September day, a bull left the Rebel lines and walked through a cornfield, stopping in front of the Fourteenth Connecticut. The men detailed to eliminate the bull had difficulty hitting their target—they fired so many rounds that officers thought the Rebels were firing at them and called out the First Brigade for assistance in what could only be called the "Third Battle of Bull Run." The tempers of angered and aggrieved officers were calmed, it was noted, with "liberal portions of the animal."

The war continued, and the Fourteenth Connecticut continued in the thick of the fighting, at the Wilderness, Spotsylvania, Ream's Station and more. Lieutenant Schalk was struck down at Spotsylvania and Franklin Nickels at Ream's Station.

NORWICH IN THE FOURTEENTH CONNECTICUT

James Bolles Coit

James Bolles Coit was born in Norwich in 1838, the son of sea captain William W. Coit and his wife, Nancy Ann Bolles Coit. He trained as a lawyer and spent time in western states, returning home when the war broke out.

With Frank Chester, he raised the first company from Norwich, enlisted as a private with the Second Connecticut regiment and had been promoted to sergeant major by the time they mustered out.

Coit reenlisted as a first lieutenant of Company K in the Fourteenth Connecticut. Although he missed the Battle of Gettysburg because of his injury, he fought with the regiment for the next year and was wounded several times. In reports on the Battle of Ream's Station in August 1864, Major Coit was specifically mentioned for gallantry in the field. He was wounded and forced to resign as a result of the subsequent disability. Coit was promoted to major and subsequently brevetted colonel and, ultimately, brigadier general in March 1865.

After the war, he returned to Norwich and married Annie Willoughby, with whom he had four children. They lived with her foster parents on

Washington Street near Christ Church. He resumed his legal practice, specializing in patents. When he died in 1894, General Coit was buried at Arlington National Cemetery.

Henry Perkins Goddard

Henry Goddard was the son of Levi Hart and Mary (Perkins) Goddard. His father was an attorney, and his grandfather was a congressman. After graduating from Norwich Free Academy, young Goddard became a reporter at the *Norwich Bulletin*, where his assignments included covering Abraham Lincoln's 1860 visit to Norwich.

Goddard first enlisted in a cavalry unit but resigned after a short time. In June 1862, he enlisted in the Fourteenth Connecticut Infantry as sergeant major of the regiment but, within two months, was promoted to second lieutenant. Goddard's diaries and letters home were preserved and passed down in his family. They were recently published in a book titled *The Good Fight That Didn't End* and provide an eye-opening account of life in the army from the perspective of a soldier on the front lines. While recuperating from a wound, Goddard also spent some time on the staff of General Daniel Tyler.

After the war, Goddard went into the insurance business and left Norwich for Hartford, where he was married to Louise Marston. After her death, he married Lida W. Acheson, with whom he had one son. The Goddards moved to Baltimore, Maryland, where Henry died in 1916 at the age of seventy-eight. He is buried in Arlington National Cemetery.

10

Brothers in Arms

Throughout the war, there were families with more than one boy in the fight. Sometimes they were brothers, sometimes cousins. Usually, the Norwich boys fought for the Union, but in at least four Norwich families, brother fought against brother. These four families are representative of the way the war affected families, not only in Norwich but across the nation.

The McCalls

Stephen and Judith Ann McCall lived in Yantic, a small village in the northern part of Norwich. Stephen McCall was a carpenter, and Judith was a homemaker. They had four children—two boys and two girls.

By the time their eldest son, John, was sixteen, he was working as a machinist, perhaps in the Yantic Woolen Mill, where most of the village men worked. He later began working for the railroad, and by 1860, John McCall was an engineer on the Hartford, Fishkill and Providence line.

Asa Dwight McCall, who was called Dwight, was five years younger than his brother and worked as a machinist as well.

John and Dwight were members of the Yantic Fire Engine Company, the volunteer fire department that served the village and the surrounding area. Most of the members worked at the mill, as owner Erastus Williams had established the fire company to provide protection for his property.

John A. McCall

Captain John A. McCall. *Author's collection.*

John McCall was twenty-six when he enlisted as a private in Company D of the Eighth Connecticut Regiment in August 1861. He was elected sergeant and marched off with his regiment a month later. His regiment fought with Burnside in North Carolina. In the summer of 1862, it was ordered to Virginia with the Army of the Potomac, and in September, it was at Antietam.

Sergeant McCall had been promoted to lieutenant that August, and with his company, he was at the extreme left flank of the Union line. Although unsupported by other Union troops, soldiers of the Eighth were able to advance to within a few rods of Rebel troops despite what was described as "withering" fire. Newspaper accounts indicate Sergeant McCall was wounded in the thigh and taken prisoner but immediately paroled.

McCall survived his Antietam wound, and after he was exchanged, he rejoined his regiment. McCall was described as a man who "possessed all the prominent characteristics of a good officer" and was known for his bravery and skilful management of his men. Another promotion in February 1863 made him captain in command of Company K.

At the Siege of Suffolk on April 15, 1863, it was John McCall who leapt from a gunboat and led two hundred men across the Nasemond River in broad daylight to storm and capture Fort Huger. McCall and his company were ordered "to take and hold the rifle pits, commanding the approach to the Fort. He was the first man to reach the land, and his part was strictly and gallantly performed."

McCall's luck ran out a year later at Drewry's Bluff (Fort Darling) near Richmond, Virginia. On May 16, 1864, Captain McCall was sitting on the ground when a bullet struck his heart. Witnesses said McCall stood, declared, "I am a dead man," and fell backward, quite dead.

Twenty-seven-year-old McCall was buried with full military and Masonic honors at a funeral attended by, among others, the Norwich Common

Council, which had passed resolutions recognizing his bravery. A family history describes the testimonial of McCall's colleagues at the Hartford, Providence and Fishkill Railroad, who sent a letter of condolence and a "handsome sum" of money toward a suitable monument in his memory.

Asa Dwight McCall

Just three months after John left, the McCalls watched another son go off to the war. Twenty-three-year-old Dwight enlisted as a first lieutenant in Company G of the Twelfth Connecticut Infantry regiment, one of the few Norwich men, and the sole commissioned officer from the city.

After it left Connecticut on December 3, 1861, the Twelfth spent most of its service in Louisiana and Virginia and saw action at Port Hudson and in the Shenandoah Valley, as well as a number of other locations.

Lieutenant McCall was wounded on October 19, 1864, at Cedar Creek, Virginia, the regiment's last major battle. He was honourably discharged in November and came home to Norwich. He married his wife, Harriet, on March 4, 1864, apparently during the time the regiment was on veteran furlough.

Dwight went into business with his brother-in-law Nelson Robinson, husband of the McCall boys' eldest sister, Amoret. In the 1860 census, Nelson Robinson and his wife were living with the McCalls. Nelson's

Dwight McCall certificate. *Courtesy of Yantic Fire Engine Company No. 1.*

occupation was given as "wheelwright." By 1868, the Robinsons were living on their own at 8 Sherman Street, and Dwight and Nelson had opened Robinson & McCall, carriage makers, at Lafayette Square near the Falls. Dwight McCall's address isn't clear; there is no separate residential listing for him. He was first lieutenant and treasurer of the Buckingham Guards militia unit in Norwich.

In 1867, the Connecticut General Assembly issued certificates recognizing the service of the state's citizen soldiers. The certificate received by Dwight McCall hangs in a place of honor at the Yantic firehouse.

By 1870, thirty-two-year-old Dwight was living in Norwich with his wife, Harriet, twenty-six, and their daughter, Eula, age one. Their first child, a boy, lived only a day after his birth in 1866. Four years later, Dwight and Harriet had moved to Washington, D.C., where he was working at the Department of the Interior as a clerk in the land office. He was apparently joining his other sister, Sarah, and her husband, Lewis Edward Forrest Spofford, who had moved to Washington in late 1870 or early 1871.

L.E. Forrest Spofford

Lewis Edward Spofford, who was always identified in records as L.E. Forrest Spofford, served with John McCall in the Eighth Regiment. A graduate of Norwich Free Academy, Spofford was only eighteen when he enlisted in September 1861. He was wounded in a charge at Antietam and lost his left arm and was wounded again at Walthall Junction. He rejoined his regiment until the end of his three years' enlistment. Although he wanted to reenlist, he was invalided out in November 1864. At his discharge, he was sergeant major of the regiment. He married Sarah McCall on August 11, 1867, and they had a daughter, Lilian, born in 1876.

In Norwich, Spofford was, for several years, assistant librarian at the Otis Library. In Washington, he was a clerk at the land office. He died on September 16, 1878.

Within a few years, things appeared to go downhill for Dwight McCall. The 1880 census for Washington shows forty-three-year-old McCall, a soldier who was born in Connecticut, as an inmate at St. Elizabeth's Hospital for the Insane. St. Elizabeth's was apparently a haven for soldiers suffering what would today be called posttraumatic stress disorder.

His daughter died in 1880 at eleven years of age, followed by her mother in 1883. Although records show Dwight McCall's death in Washington on November 17, 1898, his whereabouts for the previous eighteen years are uncertain. No listing appears for him in the city directory for either Washington or Norwich during the 1880s. His body was brought to Norwich for burial.

Sarah Spofford stayed on in Washington until at least 1900 and, by 1920, was living in Norwich with her sister, Amoret Robinson. She died on December 5, 1920.

The Goddards

Goddard family members had been prominent in Norwich affairs for many years, and their business and social connections were widespread. Calvin Goddard had been mayor of Norwich, a state representative, a U.S. congressman and a judge in the early part of the nineteenth century. Many of the city's best attorneys, including Senator Lafayette S. Foster, had read law with Calvin Goddard. His wife, Alice Hart Goddard, was the daughter of a well-known minister from the nearby town of Preston.

His son, Levi Hart Goddard, was a well-known lawyer in his own right. After graduating from Yale and passing the bar, he practiced law for a time in Ohio before returning to Connecticut. He and his wife, Mary Woodbridge Perkins, lived on a farm in Salem before returning to Norwich, where he practiced law until his death in 1862.

Henry Perkins Goddard

Henry Goddard was the third child of Levi and Mary Woodbridge (Perkins) Goddard. After his graduation from Norwich Free Academy, he became a reporter for the local newspaper, the *Norwich Bulletin*.

Rather than join any of the local regiments when he enlisted in 1862, Goddard enlisted in the cavalry. Although the unit mustered in Hartford, it was incorporated into the New York unit known as the Harris Light Cavalry, which ultimately became the Second Regiment of New York Volunteer Cavalry. Companies C and D became known as the Connecticut Squadron because so many Nutmeggers were on their rolls. Goddard resigned after about two months, primarily because of his father's death.

Goddard's experiences in the army were documented in a journal and in letters sent to family members, who were asked to keep the missives so they could be used later to complete Goddard's records.

When the Fourteenth Connecticut Volunteer Infantry was being organized later in 1862, Goddard enlisted again. This time, he was commissioned sergeant major of the regiment. He continued to send articles to the *Bulletin* and other newspapers describing his experiences. Goddard declined an offer from a New York paper to be a war correspondent; he preferred to fight.

Goddard was at Antietam and Fredericksburg, where he saved the life of Colonel Sanford Perkins. He was wounded and spent part of his recuperation on the staff of General Daniel Tyler, causing him to miss the Battle of Gettysburg. He interviewed others, though, and was able to create an account of Pickett's Charge that *Harper's Weekly* was happy to publish.

Health issues brought a permanent departure from the army in the spring of 1864. After the war, Goddard pursued a career in insurance in Hartford, where he was a neighbor and friend of Samuel Langhorne Clemens (Mark Twain). His first wife died, and by 1882, Goddard had remarried and moved to Baltimore, Maryland. Goddard and his second wife had a son, Calvin Hooker Goddard, who became a doctor. Later in his life, Calvin H. Goddard was well known for his work in forensic science, especially ballistics.

Captain Henry Goddard died of pneumonia in 1916 at the age of seventy-three. His sister Julia had married John Piatt in 1859. After the war, the youngest sister, Mary (May), would marry Louis Comfort Tiffany, son of the well-known New York jeweler.

Alfred Mitchell Goddard

Alfred M. Goddard. *Courtesy of the Faith Trumbull Chapter of the Daughters of the American Revolution.*

The week before John McCall was laid to rest in May 1864, Levi and Mary Goddard buried their eldest son, Alfred Mitchell Goddard. Alfred was born in 1836.

In 1860, a newspaper story profiled Alfred as governor of the Phenix Guano Islands in the South Pacific, where he was apparently overseeing the guano harvesting operations. Although his brother Henry, who was already in the thick of the fighting, tried to discourage his enlistment, Alfred joined the Eighth Connecticut Infantry, where he was commissioned a lieutenant.

Lieutenant Goddard saw only one battle. He was rallying his men near Petersburg when he was struck. The Goddards were prominent enough that the *Hartford Courant*, which circulated forty miles from Norwich, reported that he had been wounded, and his mother and brother were heading to the hospital at Fortress Monroe in Virginia.

The Norwich City Council attended the funeral, and at the next meeting, members adopted a series of resolutions to "express our high regard for him as a citizen" and also to assure his mother they shared her grief.

Calvin Goddard

Henry and Alfred Goddard's cousin Calvin Goddard—second son of James B. Goddard and his wife, Jane Newton Adams—enlisted as a first lieutenant with the Twelfth Ohio Infantry. He became an aide-de-camp on the staff of General Rosecrans in January 1862. By November, Rosecrans had been promoted to major general, and Lieutenant Goddard had been promoted to major.

He was subsequently promoted to the rank of lieutenant colonel in January 1863 and resigned from the army the following October.

Francis Adams Goddard

Perhaps it was the influence of his Virginia-born mother or her family, or perhaps he liked being different—there's really no way to tell why Frank Goddard eschewed the Union army to enlist in a Confederate unit.

Frank Goddard was born in Norwich in 1836, the eldest son of James and Jane Goddard. His father and Levi Goddard were brothers, making him a cousin to Henry and Alfred. In 1850, James Goddard was living with his family in New Rochelle, New York, where "Custom House" was given as his occupation. Besides his parents, the family included Frank's brothers Calvin, then twelve, and William, five.

Jane Adams was born near Alexandria, Virginia, where her father was a prominent merchant. During Jane's childhood years, Francis Adams had been U.S. consul in Austria and consular agent in Cuba, where he established a coffee plantation.

Jane Adams was seventeen when she married James Goddard in 1833. By contrast, her sister Mary, four years younger, was nearly thirty when she

Left: Frank Goddard. *Courtesy of the Faith Trumbull Chapter of the Daughters of the American Revolution.*

Below: Frank Goddard's grave. *Photo by Barry Wilson.*

married Gardiner Greene, whose family lived just down Washington Street from the Goddard's Sachem Street home.

It appears that Frank Goddard's original enlistment was in Company G of the Third Alabama Infantry—known as the Montgomery "Free Blues." Colonel J.M. Withers formed the regiment in 1861 with membership mainly drawn from Montgomery and Mobile. They fought at Seven Pines and then Malvern Hill, suffering heavy losses. After a year, part of Company G, including Goddard, was transferred to an artillery unit.

Little is known about Frank Goddard until the time of his death, which was recorded on August 17, 1884, in New York City. The death certificate indicated he was married and gave his occupation as clerk. He was brought home to Norwich to be buried in Yantic Cemetery, not far from his cousin Alfred's grave. The Stars and Bars is placed near Goddard's gravestone in May when local residents decorate the graves of Civil War veterans.

The Arms Brothers

The Reverend Hiram Phelps Arms was pastor of First Congregational Church on the Norwichtown Green for nearly forty years. He was known as an abolitionist preacher and had been asked to officiate at the funeral of Aaron Dwight Stevens, who was hanged for treason after Harper's Ferry.

Reverend Arms was twice married and had sons in each marriage. Three of his sons fought for the Union; a fourth fought for the Confederacy.

Charles Jessup Arms

The reports were not good for Charlie Arms in his second year at Yale. He started at Yale in the fall of 1859 but had been only a fair student. As a junior, Charlie had earned enough demerits to warrant suspension for the spring semester.

Charlie Arms, a son of the Reverend Arms and his second wife, was born in Norwich in 1841. He enlisted as adjutant of the Twentieth Connecticut in August 1862. By November, he had been promoted to captain. He was transferred to the staff of Brigadier General Harland and served with Harland in Virginia and North Carolina until he mustered out in June 1865.

After the war, Arms returned to his studies and read law, perhaps being influenced by General Harland, who was a lawyer. He spent some time as a lawyer in Pennsylvania before he became interested in journalism and worked at papers in Pennsylvania. Yale awarded him honorary bachelor's and master's degrees in 1875. In 1873, Arms married Alice Avery of Cincinnati, Ohio, with whom he had four children. By 1886, Charlie Arms had moved his family to East Greenwich, Rhode Island, where he worked for a short time at the *Providence Journal*, and then returned to the practice of law. He died in March 1901 and is buried in Norwich's Yantic Cemetery.

Frank H. Arms

Frank H. Arms was commissioned in 1864 as acting assistant paymaster in the U.S. Navy aboard the USS *Memphis*. He was promoted to paymaster with the rank of major in 1871, according to Reverend Dana's records.

He married Grace Turner, and she and their children apparently lived with her parents in New London as Frank remained in the navy after the war ended. Frank Arms was killed at age fifty-two in the 1889 wreck of the USS *Vandalia* when it sank in Samoa during a cyclone.

George Henry Arms

George Henry Arms was born in 1833, the middle son of Reverend Hiram Arms and his first wife, Lucy Ann Wadhams. Little infomation has been discovered about George's life before the war, but it appears he married young, to Henrietta Mackay, a Kentucky native whose family had strong Virginia roots. They apparently lived in Norwich for a while, since the Rose City is listed as the birthplace for their first son, Hiram, in 1855. The family was in Kentucky by 1857 when the second child, Sophia, was born. By 1861, they were in Alabama, where Julia was born.

George Arms may have volunteered to join the Confederate army, or he may have been subject to a draft that required military service for all eligible males. In any case, George, who had been trained as an engineer, was listed as a captain of engineers in the Confederate army rolls, although no specific regiment was given. It is said he was known as "Bridge Builder" Arms.

The circumstances are unknown, but the couple was in Mississippi for Frederick's birth about 1864. After the war, they apparently settled in Pennsylvania, where Charles was born about 1866. The family was enumerated in Lewistown in the 1870 census.

George Arms died in Boston in 1878, and by 1880, Henrietta—identified as "Hettie"—and her children were living with her widowed father-in-law. He died in 1882, leaving Hettie in need of a way to support herself. She turned to nursing and became nurse, companion and friend to famed novelist Harriet Beecher Stowe, who lived in Hartford. When Hettie Arms died in 1900, newspapers across the country carried her obituary. One described her as "Southern to the core" and a "hater of all things Northern" who was nevertheless a friend and companion to the author of *Uncle Tom's Cabin*.

THE ROCKWELLS

Two bothers from this prominent Norwich family enlisted in the army during the war. They were the sons of former congressman John A. Rockwell, who had been a state senator, lawyer and judge who was often in Washington, D.C. Their mother was Mary Watkinson Perkins, herself a member of an illustrious family. There were three sons: John Arnold (1829), Alfred Perkins (1834) and Joseph Perkins (1843).

The family lived in the house built by Mary's father on what is now Rockwell Street in Norwich, but after her husband's death, Mary closed up the house and took her sons Alfred and Joseph to live at the fashionable Wauregan House in downtown Norwich. John became a doctor; the two younger boys joined the army before embarking on careers.

Alfred Perkins Rockwell

Alfred P. Rockwell. *Courtesy of the Faith Trumbull Chapter of the Daughters of the American Revolution.*

Alfred Rockwell graduated from Yale and then stayed to earn a master's degree in 1858, which he followed with the traditional grand tour of Europe. He spent additional time in England and Germany, studying geology and metallurgy and visiting collieries to learn about modern mining technology and the economics of the coal industry.

When the war began, he returned to the United States to enlist as a captain in the First Connecticut Light Artillery in January 1862. Two years later, Rockwell was promoted to colonel and given command of the Sixth Connecticut Infantry. Later, he was brevetted brigadier general.

Rockwell was on the board of visitors at West Point for a short time before joining the faculty at Yale. A few years later, he was invited to join the faculty at Massachusetts Institute of Technology in Cambridge, Massachusetts.

In 1872, a fire destroyed much of downtown Boston, and Rockwell was appointed chairman of Boston's board of fire commissioners. He left MIT to serve as president of the Eastern Railroad from 1876 to 1879 and then became treasurer of the Great Falls Manufacturing Company in New Hampshire and remained there until he retired in 1886.

Rockwell and his wife, Katherine Foote, lived in Boston until they moved to the Massachusetts North Shore. They had three children, but only one reached adulthood.

Joseph Perkins Rockwell

Joseph P. Rockwell. *Courtesy of the Faith Trumbull Chapter of the Daughters of the American Revolution.*

Joseph Rockwell graduated from Norwich Free Academy and then took what a family genealogy described as "an extended sea voyage," which placed him overseas when the war began. He came home in time to join the Eighteenth Connecticut Infantry as it was being formed. Joe enlisted as sergeant major but was soon promoted to captain.

He was among the men captured a month later at the Second Battle of Winchester and spent nine months at Libby Prison.

After he mustered out at the end of the war, Joe Rockwell entered Yale and graduated from the Scientific School in 1868, having trained as a civil engineer. He was involved with railroad construction in Connecticut before joining the Chicago, Burlington and Quincy railroad, where he was promoted to assistant superintendent.

He moved to Texas in 1876 to become manager of the North Texas Cotton Company, but the climate aggravated health problems he had contracted in the army, so he returned to Norwich about 1880. Joe Rockwell, who had remained a bachelor, died in 1885 while visiting Boston, where records showed the cause of death as liver disease.

11

The Women's War

When the first soldiers marched to the train that would take them to the war, the downtown streets were lined with citizens. Some came to witness the event while others wanted to show their support for "our boys." Others were caught up in the excitement of it all. Banners and flags were hung on nearly every building. A band would have been playing military airs and, almost certainly, "The Girl I Left Behind Me" as white handkerchiefs fluttered in the hands of female onlookers.

It's not hard to imagine the women's collective sigh as the troop train pulled out of the Norwich depot, followed by a brisk declaration that it was time to get to work. The government might provide weapons and uniforms, but it was up to the city's women to furnish the comforts that would make the soldiers' rough lives bearable.

Their work had begun the day of the mass war meeting in Breed Hall, where the women took over the balconies and offices to sew uniforms for Captain Chester's company. They continued sewing on Sunday, April 21, breaking the ironclad rule that prohibited labor on Sunday, but no one appeared to mind, considering the circumstances and the grave national crisis that was at hand.

The women of the town were credited with making 1,600 flannel and checked cotton shirts, as well as "other articles of apparel required by the soldiers for their outfit." As they sewed, the ladies sang to help pass the time. A favorite was composed by one of the women, identified only by her initials, which were E.P., according to Reverend Dana, who noted that

E.P. later became a leader of the Soldiers' Aid group. The initials strongly suggest the author was Eliza Perkins, who was, in fact, one of the Soldiers' Aid group leaders. The first performance of the composition was the day Captain Chester's men left Norwich. A "choir of young ladies" stood on the balcony of the Wauregan House (today's Wauregan Hotel) to sing the verses, which included:

Our flag to our eyes is the emblem
Of all that the soul holds most dear!
To defend it, we'll show the proud boaster,
Northern men neither tremble nor fear!
In such danger 'tis no time to dally.
We'll swear to be faithful anew;
Party names all forgetting, we'll rally.
'Round the flag of the red, white and blue.

Perhaps the greatest contribution of the women of Norwich was the Soldiers' Aid Society formed in September 1861 in response to a request for woolen stockings (knee-high socks) for the soldiers. With donated yarn, the ladies began to knit. Warm socks were a necessity, especially for a soldier. Although it was possible to obtain them, most people at the time considered factory-knitted (by machine) socks and stockings inferior to the hand-knitted items. Publications such as Godey's *Lady's Book* published patterns for making stockings suitable for the soldiers, and early in 1865, the U.S. Sanitary Commission distributed an "official" pattern that met military specifications, which was widely published. Also published were patterns for knitted hospital slippers.

The October 26, 1861 issue of *Scientific American* contained these instructions:

THE WAR.
The government calls upon the loyal women of America to knit stockings for our brave soldiers. The following rules are laid down for the direction of ladies wishing to knit socks for the soldiers:—Get large needles and a coarse yarn; cast on seventy-eight stitches, and knit the leg ten inches before setting the heel. The heel should be three and a half inches long, and knit of double yarn, one fine and one coarse, for extra strength. The foot should be eleven or twelve inches long.

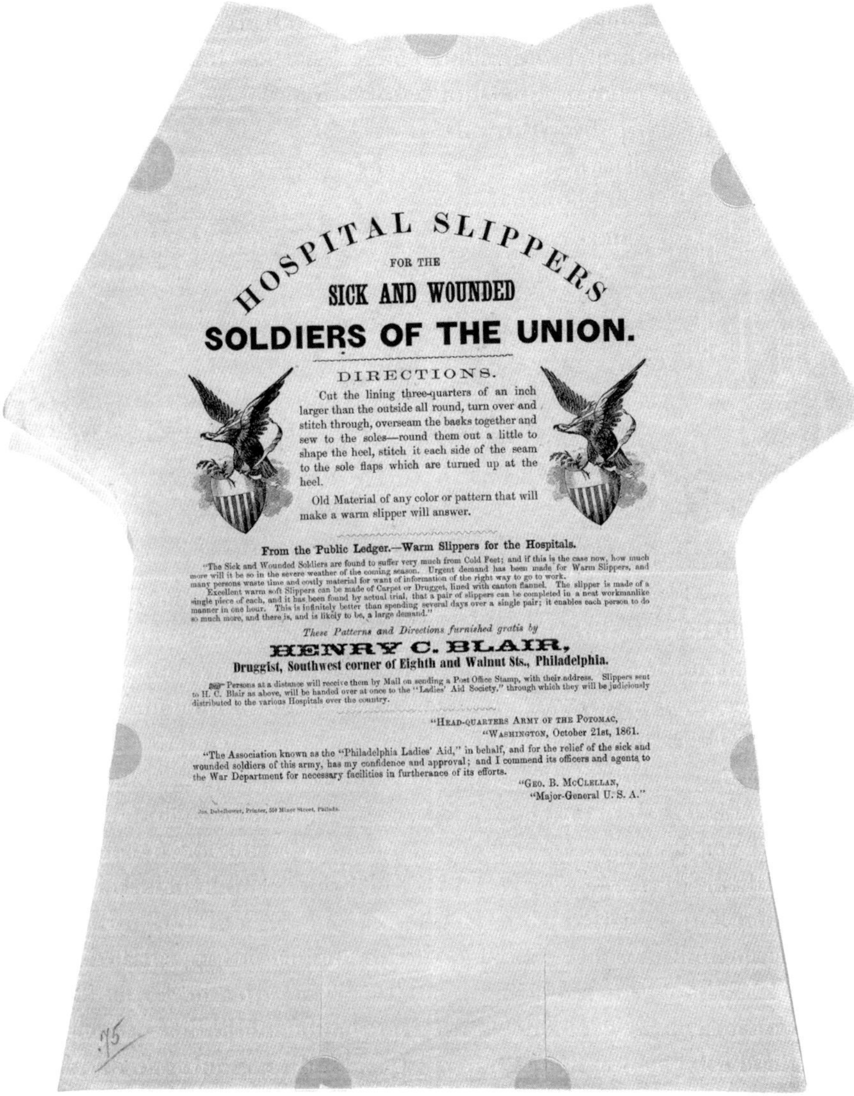

HOSPITAL SLIPPERS
FOR THE
SICK AND WOUNDED
SOLDIERS OF THE UNION.

DIRECTIONS.

Cut the lining three-quarters of an inch larger than the outside all round, turn over and stitch through, overseam the backs together and sew to the soles—round them out a little to shape the heel, stitch it each side of the seam to the sole flaps which are turned up at the heel.

Old Material of any color or pattern that will make a warm slipper will answer.

From the Public Ledger.—Warm Slippers for the Hospitals.

"The Sick and Wounded Soldiers are found to suffer very much from Cold Feet; and if this is the case now, how much more will it be so in the severe weather of the coming season. Urgent demand has been made for Warm Slippers, and many persons waste time and costly material for want of information of the right way to go to work.

Excellent warm soft Slippers can be made of Carpet or Drugget, lined with canton flannel. The slipper is made of a single piece of each, and it has been found by actual trial, that a pair of slippers can be completed in a neat workmanlike manner in one hour. This is infinitely better than spending several days over a single pair; it enables each person to do so much more, and there is, and is likely to be, a large demand."

These Patterns and Directions furnished gratis by

HENRY C. BLAIR,
Druggist, Southwest corner of Eighth and Walnut Sts., Philadelphia.

Persons at a distance will receive them by Mail on sending a Post Office Stamp, with their address. Slippers sent to H. C. Blair as above, will be handed over at once to the "Ladies' Aid Society," through which they will be judiciously distributed to the various Hospitals over the country.

"HEAD-QUARTERS ARMY OF THE POTOMAC,
"WASHINGTON, October 21st, 1861.

"The Association known as the "Philadelphia Ladies' Aid," in behalf, and for the relief of the sick and wounded soldiers of this army, has my confidence and approval; and I commend its officers and agents to the War Department for necessary facilities in furtherance of its efforts.

"GEO. B. MCCLELLAN,
"Major-General U. S. A."

Jas. Debelhower, Printer, 510 Minor Street, Philada.

Broadside of a pattern for hospital slippers for the sick and wounded soldiers of the Union. *Courtesy of the Library of Congress. Printed Ephemera Collection; Portfolio 157, Folder 22. DIGITAL ID rbpe 15702200.*

During the four years of the war, records kept by the Soldiers' Aid Society show 6,587 pairs of stockings were sent to the front.

The ranks of the knitters included women in their nineties, like a Mrs. Cady of Norwich Falls and Mrs. Thomas Lathrop of Norwich Town, aged ninety-two, and a ninety-one-year-old woman from nearby Lisbon, who contributed both stockings and mittens. Another knitter kept track of her production but didn't share the tally with anyone. After her death, her family found this note, dated July 4, 1864:

> *To-day, the anniversary of our glorious independence, I have completed the one hundredth pair of socks that I have knitted for the brave soldiers, who are nobly sustaining the honor of our country on many a hard fought battle-field. God grant them success. Theirs will be the glory when the Stars and Stripes wave over a united nation.*

Another important role for the Soldiers' Aid Society was supplying regimental hospitals. At the suggestion of Governor Buckingham, hospitals for the Sixth, Eighth, Eleventh and Thirteenth Regiments became the province of the Norwich women. They invited women from Windham County and the rest of New London County to join them in meeting the soldiers' needs.

Elizabeth Greene, known as Lizzie, became head of the Soldiers' Aid Society. She was the eldest daughter of Norwich textile manufacturer William P. Greene. Unmarried at thirty-seven, she had the time and the means to make a significant contribution to the war effort.

Her family owned the Falls and Shetucket companies, and it was for the Greene family that the village of Greeneville was named. Her father had been mayor in 1841; her brother James Lloyd Greene was first elected mayor in 1861 and was reelected throughout the war.

Lizzie Greene was, by all accounts, what we would today call a "dynamo" who apparently shared the family talent for organization, leadership and the other skills needed to run a successful business venture.

Her "untiring zeal and personal superintendence" was critical in bringing the Norwich Soldiers' Aid Society to its "efficiency and widening scope, which made it second to no other kindred association in the State" while her "executive skill and womanly tact" kept up the interest in and maintained community support for the society's work. She became known as "the soldier's friend"…because "she made the sympathy and help of Norwich women felt by Connecticut troops wherever they were to be found, in camp, hospital, or prison."

A number of the Greene family's personal connections were at the front. Their across-the-street neighbor was General Daniel Tyler. Lizzie's sister, Augusta, became engaged to Colonel William G. Ely, and surely the family would have worried over him when he was captured and taken to Libby Prison in Virginia.

The Greenes' neighbors also included William and Eliza Aiken and John T. Almy. Since Almy was the state's agent in New York, seeing to the needs of any Connecticut soldier who came through the city, his work with the New England Soldiers' Relief Association in New York would almost certainly have been a topic of conversation when they met.

For most of the war, two other women worked with Lizzie Greene to ensure that the Soldiers' Aid Society operations went smoothly. Caroline L. "Carrie" Thomas was the daughter of Henry Thomas, a wealthy New York merchant whose family originated in Norwich. He came to the city about 1828 and purchased the Thomas Lathrop house (385 Washington Street) in Norwich. Carrie's mother was active in the Norwich Town's women's aid group known as the Nightingales.

Eliza P. Perkins was the forty-five-year-old daughter of Francis A. and Abby Perkins, who lived on Union Street. Her father was treasurer of the Norwich Savings Society. After her father's death in 1864, Miss Perkins moved to Upper Washington Street in Norwich.

Later in the war, they were joined by Emmeline Norton, one of the twin daughters of Henry B. and Emmeline Norton. Her father, a wholesale grocer and promoter of the Norwich steamship line, was himself one of the mainstays of the Norwich war effort.

Around the same time as the Norwich aid society was forming, Mrs. Henry Thomas (Caroline's mother) and Mrs. Daniel W. Coit organized a sister group in Norwich, called the Nightingales. Carrie Thomas worked with her mother and acted as what was described as a "sort of secretary" who kept track of contributions to the main aid society.

Women from other sections of Norwich contributed as well. The ladies of Greeneville supported the effort throughout the war but were especially proud of the supplies they sent to the Norwich men held captive at the Libby and Belle Isle Prisons.

After regiments for African American soldiers were established, the city's African American women organized an aid society with Mrs. Walter Burr at its head. Their mission was to provide comforts to the men of the Twenty-ninth and Thirtieth Regiments. Their records were lost, so there is no statistical information about their work, although they did much for the welfare of the men they watched over.

Early in the war, the U.S. Sanitary Commission was formed and established a national effort to provide soldiers' comforts. If local agencies would do the collecting, the national agency would distribute items to where they were most needed. So many boxes came from Norwich that people in other areas thought the Norwich aid society much larger than it was. Norwich contributions were delivered to the Soldiers' Aid Society headquarters in the Rockwell Building in downtown Norwich. There, the contents were regrouped, packed in boxes and then shipped in response to the requests that came from all over the country.

The Norwich ladies sent the first box of supplies received by the First Regiment South Carolina Volunteers, whose members were former slaves fighting for the Union. In addition to the boxes sent to the hospitals under their special charge, boxes from Norwich arrived at military hospitals and also several freedmen's hospitals.

Soldiers' Aid Society records tallied the items sent to the troops. These included quilts, blankets, pillows, pillowcases and sheets. In addition to mittens and stockings, shirts were a major clothing item that were needed, as was the means to mend damage, in the form of pincushions and thread bags.

Not only were the ladies making every article that was sent away, but they also had to raise the money for materials. During 1861, the Soldiers' Aid Society reported contributions totaling $426.92. For 1862, contributions were $3,369.04 and included $344 realized from three concerts and $55 from the Lyceum Lecture Committee. By 1863, receipts had fallen off, with $2,142.54 reported for the year, including $50 from the noted abolitionist

THE ORGANIZATIONS SUPPLIED BY THE AID SOCIETY.

Forwarded to the	Quilts.	Pillows.	Bed Sacks.	Blankets.	Pillow Cases.	Wrappers.	Drawers.	Flannel Shirts.	Socks.	Sheets.	Towels.	Slippers.	Mittens.	Handkerchiefs.	Cotton Shirts.	Packages of Sundries.
Woman's Central Relief Association	279	243	74	–	305	73	471	1,265	1,618	463	339	204	–	–	512	352 and 1 barrel jellies, dried apples, etc.
Sixth Regiment	–	–	–	–	–	–	–	–	–	–	–	–	74	–	–	–
Eighth Regiment	85	62	–	61	100	42	248	337	786	81	249	–	146	45	157	60
Eleventh Regiment	36	–	49	8	33	–	24	40	76	74	38	–	–	–	–	59
Thirteenth Regiment	115	–	102	75	100	–	120	56	79	144	75	–	195	–	–	140 and 1 hhd. London porter.
Fourteenth Regiment	–	12	12	–	–	–	18	–	24	26	64	–	–	–	–	5
Eighteenth Regiment	–	21	21	–	15	18	–	158	154	55	52	–	–	–	–	71
Twenty-first Regiment	–	–	18	–	–	18	48	48	42	72	60	–	–	–	–	–
New England Woman's Aid Association	186	105	–	–	50	–	22	232	–	48	26	12	–	25	–	258 and 8 vests.
Fairfax Hospital, Alexandria, Va.	–	–	–	–	–	–	8	–	42	–	18	4	–	36	39	–
David's Island Hospital	–	–	–	–	–	1	–	132	73	–	12	–	–	–	4	Dried apples and wine and 24 thread and needle bags.
First Conn. Cavalry	–	–	–	–	–	–	–	–	–	–	–	–	36	–	–	1 box turkeys and 27 thread and needle bags.
Sanitary Commission	–	–	–	–	–	–	–	100	50	–	–	–	–	–	–	Old linen, blackberry syrup, and wine.
Christian Commission	–	–	–	–	–	–	–	39	29	–	–	–	–	–	–	Books and papers.
Connecticut State Agent	–	–	–	–	–	–	–	54	42	–	–	–	–	–	–	1 box wine.

Forwarded to the Freedmen: 3 quilts, 103 dresses, 24 aprons, 1 shawl, 19 under-garments, 9 coats, 11 vests, 8 pants, 2 hats, 1 pair boots 16 shirts, 7 barrels clothing, books and papers.

A table showing items produced by the Norwich Soldier's Aid Society. *Author's collection.*

Wendell Phillips. Some records have been lost, but the best available information recorded $1,191.25 from November 1864 to September 1865.

Over the four years of war, the aid society spent more than $3,000 for flannel and another $1,300 for "sheeting, shirting and calico," and more than $1,000 for yarn. Apparently, some cash contributions were made, including $128 to needy soldiers and families, $25 to the Connecticut State Agent and $65 to the David's Island Hospital. In total, the society had expenditures of $7,909. At the end of the war, whatever remained was used to benefit "needy soldiers and their families."

Anyone who had doubts about a woman's ability to organize and execute a major fundraiser need only consider the September 1862 fair at Christ Church. The ladies netted $710 for the Soldiers' Aid Society, which would be about $212,000 in 2013.

For most of a week in April 1864, Breed Hall was home to an exhibition to benefit the work of the Soldiers' Aid Society. The organizers planned a different activity for each evening, and the townspeople turned out for elaborately costumed characters in tableaux, charades and statuary, many of which were original designs or compositions for the event. These were accompanied by songs of some of the city's talented singers or music by White's Band. More than fifty residents, both men and women, were featured in what was considered the "most artistic and successful" such event the city had ever seen. Large crowds and enthusiastic applause greeted the effort, and the exhibition committee was able to turn over nearly $900—close to a $250,000 in 2013 dollars—to the Soldiers' Aid Society.

Committee members Gertrude May, Mrs. David Young, Emmeline Norton, Hannah Ripley, Eliza Greene, Mary Ricketts Adams Greene and Mrs. John B. Young were lauded for their "rare taste and patient labor" in arranging for the event. An interesting side note is that Mary Greene was a native Virginian and was in the position of raising money to support the soldiers fighting against men she would have known from her girlhood.

A Soldiers' Aid Society Ball early in 1864 netted $358. On election night that year, the citizens gathered to celebrate the results spontaneously raised $200 to provide comforts for the privates at the Libby Prison, who were deemed to be suffering the most.

Norwich made sure its soldiers knew they were remembered at the holidays. In 1862, the Soldiers' Aid Society was asked to provide pies for Connecticut soldiers on Long Island, and 160 pies were packed and sent off to hungry soldiers. Two years later, the society sought contributions to provide entire Thanksgiving dinners for the Connecticut regiments. The list of donations from Norwich was staggering: $574, 215 turkeys, 199 pies, thirty-three chickens, ninety-six cans of tomatoes, four and three-quarters barrels of apples, twelve tongues and forty-five bottles of pickles, as well as roast geese, spare-ribs, beef à la mode, corned beef, roast veal, brown bread, sugar, cheese, oranges, crackers, gingerbread, cake, crullers, doughnuts, cookies, gingersnaps, nuts, raisins, plum puddings and tobacco. Adams Express shipped—at no cost—twenty-one barrels and seven boxes to the local regiments. Funds were appropriated to provide turkeys for Connecticut soldiers along the James River and in the Shenandoah Valley, along with supplies for sick and wounded Connecticut men in other locations. Again, Adams Express provided shipping without cost to the aid society.

In October 1863, the Sanitary Commission sponsored the Northwestern Soldiers Fair in Chicago, and the Norwich Soldiers' Aid Society was invited to participate. When the society's contributions had been gathered, they filled a window of the Rockwell Building, where the items were displayed before they were packed up and shipped to Chicago. When the boxes arrived in Chicago, the fair organizers changed their plan to designate a separate space for Connecticut, which occupied the equivalent of two booths.

Particular notice was given in the Chicago papers to socks knitted by the arthritic hands of seventy-four-year-old Lucy Brown—her sixtieth pair—that were included with silverware, breakfast shawls, knitted items, a beadwork mat, boys' clothing and the "genuine wooden nutmegs" offered for sale at the Connecticut booth.

About halfway through the war, voluntary enlistment wasn't enough to fill out the ranks of the troops, so a draft was instituted. It was possible for a man to hire a substitute to fight in his place. For Lizzie Greene and her sister, Gussie, the Soldiers' Aid Society work wasn't enough to fulfill their patriotic feelings. Law and custom prohibited them from joining the army, but they hired substitutes to represent them in the ranks of the troops.

The government printed engraved certificates for those who provided recruits in this manner. The War Department sent the first ever issued to a Connecticut woman to Augusta Greene; another certificate was sent to Elizabeth Greene. Other women in Norwich and throughout the state followed their example.

12

1864—"We Are Proud of You"

Norwich in the Navy

Of more than eighty Norwich men who enlisted in the navy, the most illustrious was Joseph P. Lanman. In 1864–65, Commodore Lanman of Norwich led a naval division at the bombardment and capture of Fort Fisher, which controlled the entrance to the harbor at Wilmington, North Carolina.

Commodore Joseph P. Lanman. *Courtesy of the Faith Trumbull Chapter of the Daughters of the American Revolution.*

Commodore Lanman was the commander of the *Minnesota*, which was part of the North Atlantic Blocking Squadron. During the second of two attacks on the fort, Lanman and the *Minnesota* led the second line. When the battle ended, the Stars and Stripes flew over the last Confederate-controlled port. Commodore Lanman was born in Norwich and joined the navy at a young age and had assignments all over the world as he advanced in rank. He had been commodore of the Pacific Squadron early in the war.

After the war, he was commander of the North Atlantic Squadron and oversaw the dismantling of the naval wartime depots. He was also the commander of the Portsmouth, New Hampshire navy yard, where he received his commission as rear admiral in 1869. Later, he was commander of the South Atlantic Squadron off the coast of Brazil. Lanman died in 1872.

THE PROVOST MARSHAL

By the summer of 1864, the draft and hiring of substitutes had become an issue. When President Lincoln called for 300,000 more troops, the Norwich quota was 1,601, with another 273 men expected from the surrounding towns.

Captain Isaac H. Bromley, who had been assigned as provost marshal in Norwich, had the task of supervising the draft, which proved to be a thankless job. As he prepared to relinquish the post, Captain Bromley wrote:

> *The retiring officer has had the satisfaction of knowing, that in the discharge of duties eminently calculated to "make everybody hate you," he has met with the most cheering success.*
>
> *Without a pang of regret, he bids an official but affectionate adieu to the gentlemanly substitute-brokers, who have always "two or three first-rate men, of good moral character," they want to get in; to the patriotic selectmen and town agents, who would "like to look over the lists, to see if James Henry Alexander's name is down;" to the short-haired substitutes with a complication of diseases, "who swear they are tough enough to stand marching and fighting;" to the timid young gentlemen from the rural districts, who have "the rheumatism very bad in wet weather," and have never been well since the war broke out; to the anxious parties who have for the past three or four weeks waylaid him in the streets, and opened their attack with a dreadful series of "sposens"; to the aliens from Ireland, and the aliens from Germany, and the aliens who would be willing to swear they were aliens; to the mild-mannered men who "couldn't understand it"; and those rough-spoken people "who knew all about it"; to those, and to all of them, he bids a fond and affectionate farewell.*
>
> *He presumes they are all pleased with the change.*
>
> *He certainly is.*

Anticipating the presidential election, Connecticut's legislature approved a constitutional amendment that would allow soldiers in the field to vote by absentee ballot. It was put to a popular vote across the state for ratification. Although there was opposition in other parts of the state, little surfaced in New London County, and it's hard to believe anyone could have withstood the governor's declaration "that freemen who sustain and protect a government, by baring their bosoms to the deadly shafts of its enemies, should have an opportunity to express an opinion in respect to its policy, and the character and qualifications of its officers."

A newspaper commentary added the figurative exclamation point to his remarks: "Perhaps we are prejudiced, but it seems to us that a man who does nothing worse than shed his blood for the old flag ought not, for so small an offense as that, to be disfranchised like a common thief."

New London County answered affirmatively by more than 5 to 1; in Norwich, the vote was 753 to 156. The Rebel expectation that the Union army would dissipate as the three-year enlistments ran out was dashed by 40,000 draftees, 268,000 volunteers and the reenlistment of 100,000 veterans. In addition, the army organized an invalid corps of 25,000 men who would assume garrison and camp duties to free able-bodied men to go to the front. Governor Buckingham sent Colonel Selden and Captain Gallup to New Orleans to reenlist veterans among the troops formerly under their commands, and their success contributed to the 3,647 veteran reenlistments tallied by the state.

Perhaps the men acted from patriotism, perhaps for the bounty of $702 or, perhaps more importantly, the promise of a furlough. What mattered was that the army would have the benefit of their experience. As they came home on furlough, the veteran regiments found enthusiastic crowds waiting. The beautiful regimental flag might have been tattered and the fresh-faced boys had become lean, hardened, battle-weary veterans, but the Eighteenth Connecticut found a crowd waiting for them when they arrived in Norwich Harbor on March 29.

Delays meant they arrived at midnight, but there was still a crowd at the dock to cheer them and escort the regiment to the waiting banquet. As one speaker, unidentified in accounts of the event, said, "We hoped for great things from you, and I proclaim before you, that our hopes have not been disappointed. We are proud of you."

THE TWENTY-NINTH CONNECTICUT INFANTRY REGIMENT

African Americans Join the War

Following the lead of the federal government, the Connecticut General Assembly passed a bill authorizing regiments of African American soldiers in November 1863. Within ten days, Governor Buckingham put out a call for volunteers and found the response as enthusiastic as it had been for white soldiers. By January, the Twenty-ninth Regiment Colored Infantry had 1,200 recruits and more than 400 others had joined the Thirtieth Connecticut. In all, it's estimated that from 1863 to 1867, nearly 1,800 African American soldiers enlisted—roughly 78 percent of the men who were eligible to serve.

These volunteers enlisted for two years or less (depending on when the war ended). They would receive the same bounty ($600), the same pay and the same uniform as the state's other soldiers.

Norwich was represented in this regiment by David Torrance, captain (later lieutenant colonel) of Company A; M.L. Leonard and E.P. Rogers, first lieutenants of Company F; C.H. Carpenter, first lieutenant of Company K; and about twenty privates. The regiment first joined the Ninth Army Corps, proceeding to Hilton Head and Beaufort, South Carolina. Then, the unit was ordered north into the Tenth Corps. After a month in the trenches at Petersburg, the Twenty-ninth acted as the skirmish line for the division at the Battle of Fair Oakes and sustained eighty or more casualties.

Twenty-Ninth Infantry. *Courtesy of the Slater Memorial Museum.*

13

1865—Appomattox

Some historians describe the events of the first week of April 1865 as a "running battle" in which Federal troops repeatedly engaged Rebel troops as they desperately tried to escape. The last straw for Robert E. Lee may have been Sayler's Creek, where Sheridan's troops captured a Confederate supply train.

The men of the Fourteenth Connecticut counted High Bridge on April 6 and 7 as their last engagement. They set out to cross the Appomattox River at daylight and found Confederate soldiers setting the bridge on fire.

The Fourteenth Connecticut was the second regiment in line and began firing without orders as they crossed the bridge and then formed their battle line in a meadow on the other side. At nightfall, General Thomas A. Smyth, the commanding officer, was killed, becoming the regiment's final fatality of the war.

Meanwhile, at the Battle of Sailor's (or Sayler's) Creek, the clear "beginning of the end" was on the horizon for the Confederate army. The battle pitted Union troops, commanded by General Philip H. Sheridan, against the Rebel troops of Generals Richard S. Ewell and John B. Gordon.

Sailor's Creek was actually three separate simultaneous engagements in which the Union troops overwhelmed a slightly larger Confederate army and captured nearly eight thousand men—one-quarter of the remaining Confederate troops. Those captured included six confederate generals, among them Ewell and George Washington Custis Lee, the eldest son of Robert E. Lee.

April 7, 1865

Union commander Ulysses S. Grant sent to Confederate general Robert E. Lee a message suggesting that "the results of the last week must convince you of the hopelessness of further resistance." He went on to say Lee's surrender would prevent any "further effusion of blood."

Lee replied that he didn't share Grant's assessment of the situation and declined to surrender. He went on to say he shared Grant's desire to avoid more useless bloodshed and asked what terms Grant was prepared to offer if he (Lee) were to surrender.

April 8, 1865

Grant answered Lee's inquiry by emphasizing peace is "my great desire" and telling Lee he would insist on only one condition: "that the men and officers surrendered shall be disqualified for taking up arms against the government of the United States until properly exchanged." He offered to meet Lee himself or have subordinates meet, at a location of Lee's choice, to arrange terms of surrender for the Army of Northern Virginia.

In his reply, Lee emphatically stated he wasn't offering to surrender; rather, asking about the terms of surrender. He concurred, "Restoration of peace should be the sole object of all," and said he couldn't meet to surrender his army, "but as far as your proposal may affect the Confederate State forces under my command, and tend to the restoration of peace, I should be pleased to meet you at 10 o clock A.M. to-morrow."

April 9, 1865

General Grant insisted he wasn't authorized to "treat on the subject of peace" but also that he was as desirous of peace as Lee. "The terms upon which peace can be had are well understood. By the South laying down their arms, they would hasten that most desirable event…Seriously hoping that all our difficulties may be settled without the loss of another life."

Lee, who had previously insisted he wasn't contemplating surrender—although he had asked what terms might be offered—now wrote, "I now ask an interview, in accordance with the offer contained in your letter of yesterday, for that purpose [surrender of his army]."

Back with the Fourteenth Connecticut, strange events began unfolding on Sunday, April 9. Regimental historian Charles Page described the scene as the troops gained the first inkling that something momentous was happening.

Late in the morning, the regiment was ordered off the road into a field and told there would be a twenty-minute break for coffee. This was considered "suspicious," since there had been no such break for weeks. Besides, the men said, they knew enough to get breakfast without a specific order. A few got coffee; most were "too tired to care much [and] lay down to rest instead."

The twenty minutes stretched to an hour and then a second, and rumors began flying. Someone had heard there had been a proposition for surrender. Someone else had heard that Lee actually had surrendered, although those who believed that "were laughed at as credulous fools."

As it turned out, the rumors were true. The generals, Grant and Lee, met at Wilmer McLean's house at Appomattox Court House.

It's been said that for Wilmer McLean, the war started in his front yard and ended in his front parlor. In 1861, McLean, a wholesale grocer, lived on Yorkshire Plantation near Manassas Junction, Virginia. The Bull Run River ran through his land, which was the site of fighting during the first major battle of the Civil War.

Federal soldiers posing at Appomattox Court House. *Courtesy of the Library of Congress. LC-B817-7169 [P&P] LOT 4165-G.*

General Robert E. Lee surrendered his army in the front parlor of this house, the residence of Wilmer McLean. *Courtesy of the Library of Congress. LC-DIG-cwpb-03957.*

His house had been seized to be the headquarters for General P.G.T. Beauregard, the Confederate commanding officer. The detached kitchen was hit by cannonfire. McLean and his family weren't there at the time, but it was enough to persuade them to move 120 miles away to Appomattox Court House.

In an odd twist of fate, on April 9, 1865, a messenger requested the use of McLean's home for a meeting between Generals Lee and Grant. The two generals sat at separate tables in the McLean's front parlor. They spent some time chatting, and Grant reminded Lee the two had met during the Mexican War. Finally, they came to the business at hand.

Grant's terms for surrender were simple; basically, he would require the Rebels to:

- Provide a list of everyone who would be paroled.
- Turn over their weapons (officers would be allowed to keep their sidearms and horses).
- Promise not to fight against the federal government any more.
- Go home, abide by the terms of their parole and obey the laws.

Lee pointed out that the enlisted men owned their mounts, and Grant promised to arrange for them to take their animals home to work their farms. Finally, Lee offered to turn over about one thousand Union soldiers being held prisoner, since he hadn't the means to feed them. Arrangements would be made for rations for Lee's starving soldiers, who had been living on parched corn for the previous few days, and forage for the horses.

Back at the front, the men of the Fourteenth finally were convinced of the surrender when a battery of artillery closer to the rear fired a number of blank cartridges, although the volley quickly stopped. Regimental historian Page wrote:

> *General Grant refused to allow anything that looked like exultation over a fallen foe. The most extraordinary scene I think I ever witnessed was that which greeted the appearance of General Meade passing through the lines to congratulate his troops on the victory. Men were completely beside themselves: they flung their caps into the air, threw their knapsacks under his*

Troops pass the reviewing stand during the Grand Review of the Armies in Washington. *Courtesy of the Library of Congress. LC-USZ62-1731.*

Troops pass in front of the U.S. Capitol in this Matthew Brady photograph of the Grand Review of the Armies. Note the crepe hung around the windows. *Courtesy of the Library of Congress. LC-B8184-7748.*

> *horse's feet; danced and laughed and shouted and rolled on the ground and cried all at the same time. Men who declared when they went into that field, in the morning that they were so foot-sore that another step was impossible went out of that field that afternoon to the tune of Yankee Doodle, with steps as light as boys just out of school.*

The surrender of the Army of Northern Virginia meant surrender of the rest of the Confederate army wouldn't be far behind, and it seemed clear to all that Lee's surrender at Appomattox signaled the end of the war.

The Fourteenth stayed in place a few weeks and then began the two-hundred-mile march to Washington, which would include a stop in Richmond. The Fourteenth Connecticut was given the honor of marching at the head of the column of twenty thousand soldiers with the regimental band in the lead. Coming into Richmond, they passed in review before General Henry Halleck.

The march continued past places the men of the Fourteenth knew well from battles they had fought there. At Fredericksburg, "the men marched on quietly without noise, as if conscious of moving over ground sanctified by the suffering and death of their comrades."

Once they reached the outskirts of Washington, the march stopped to wait for the Grand Review of the Armies. On May 26, the Fourteenth and the rest of the column went into Washington to march with all of the other soldiers down Maryland Avenue, around the Capitol Building and up Pennsylvania Avenue and past a reviewing stand occupied by President Johnson, General Grant and others including General Winfield Scott Hancock, who was given "a royal greeting" by his former command.

A few days later, the men of the Fourteenth Connecticut boarded a train for home. As they passed through Baltimore and Philadelphia, they were greeted enthusiastically and feted; at New York, Colonel Almy, the Connecticut State agent, was on hand to greet them and provide supper and lodging for the night before he took them to the steamboat that would transport them to Hartford, where they were greeted with a hero's welcome, which included breakfast and a parade.

Then they could wait no more—they headed for the train station and home. It didn't matter that almost no one had money to pay the fare. The conductors "passed them on with a smile," the *Hartford Courant* reported.

NORWICH IN THE CAVALRY

When he went to the surrender ceremony at Appomattox, General Ulysses Grant had a cavalry escort—the riders of the First Connecticut Cavalry.

When Connecticut organized its own cavalry in the fall of 1861, the ranks of the First Regiment included several Norwich men. Among them were Charles Farnsworth, captain of Company B (later lieutenant colonel); Henry T. Phillips, second lieutenant (later first lieutenant) of Company A; and Joab B. Rogers, sergeant (later captain) of Company A. In addition, seventy-nine of the privates were Norwich men.

After leaving Norwich in January 1862, the regiment was ordered to the mountains of Virginia. In April, Captain Farnsworth was on a scouting mission with a detail of twelve men. They were in a heavily wooded area when they were ambushed by Rebel riflemen. Although Captain Farnsworth was wounded in the arm and side and all but fainting from the loss of blood, he had the presence of mind to order his men into position to counter any further attack.

Cavalry colonel Charles Farnsworth. *Courtesy of the Faith Trumbull Chapter of the Daughters of the American Revolution.*

Once recovered from the wounds, Captain Farnsworth rejoined the regiment.

In July 1863, Charlie Farnsworth, who had been promoted to major, and a unit of fifty men were ordered to scout the enemy's position near Bolivar Heights. They ran into an enemy picket line and charged, forcing the rebels back to where two hundred reserves waited. Undaunted by the size of what was now a much larger force, Major Farnsworth successfully pressed his attack, and his men captured a number of prisoners. Once the rebels realized they held the advantage in size, they regrouped and fought hand-to-hand. During the fight, Major Farnsworth's horse was shot out from under him. In the end, he and twenty-six of his men surrendered.

They spent eight months at Libby Prison, where Farnsworth found Colonel Will Ely and other Norwich friends from the Eighteenth Connecticut Infantry, who had been captured at Winchester.

When released, Farnsworth rejoined his cavalry regiment as lieutenant colonel, since he had been promoted during his imprisonment, and in May 1864, he was honorably discharged.

Around that time, the regiment was assigned to the Army of the Potomac and fought at Spotsylvania before being transferred again—this time to the Army of the Shenandoah. They rode with General Philip Sheridan and won the reputation of being "second to none" among cavalry units. Near Winchester, they captured and entire Eighth South Carolina Infantry and their colors. They fought at Winchester, Front Royal, Staunton and Waynesboro. In October, General George W. Custer was given command of the division.

At Cedar Creek on October 19, General Sheridan credited Custer's cavalry division, which included the Connecticut First, with making a charge that opened the door for the capture of artillery pieces, wagons, prisoners and flags. The Nutmeggers, who were the first to breach the Confederate lines, seized their cannon and turned it around to fire on the retreating rebels.

They survived a bitter winter in which one man froze to death in his tent, and later, fifty others were frost-bitten as the unit marched 120 miles in four days.

The First Cavalry was with Sheridan as he conducted his scorched-earth campaign throughout the Shenandoah Valley and attacked Jubal Early's headquarters, where the First led the attack. They continued on, attacking and defeating enemy troops, finally reaching Richmond.

The unit was assigned to escort General Grant to Appomattox Court House for the surrender of General Lee's army.

They saw more action with General Sheridan, and finally the unit was sent to Washington, where they participated in the Grand Review of the Armies. They remained in the capital until August on provost duty (i.e., acting as military police).

When they mustered out, members of the First Connecticut Cavalry were afforded the privilege of returning mounted, rather than marching, to Connecticut.

14

GLORY, GLORY, HALLELUJAH

The four long years of war had ended, but the joy of the victory became quite hollow on April 15, 1865. Good Friday would have new meaning for many Americans, who would mark it ever after as the day President Abraham Lincoln was shot.

LINCOLN'S ASSASSINATION

A lighthearted President Lincoln took his wife to Ford's Theater on the evening of Friday, April 14, 1865. Although the performance had already begun when they arrived, the orchestra played "Hail to the Chief" as the Lincoln party was seated in the president's box overlooking the stage. By all appearances, the president was enjoying himself, laughing heartily at the play.

At 10:15 p.m., John Wilkes Booth entered the box and fired a derringer at the back of the president's head. The unconscious Lincoln was carried to a boardinghouse across the street, where he was laid across a boarder's bed. He died at 7:22 a.m. on April 15.

Telegraph operators sprang to life as the news was flashed around the country, and the euphoria over the war's end immediately changed to gloom. The president's death meant Senator Lafayette S. Foster of Norwich had effectively become vice president of the United States. At that time, the president pro tempore of the Senate was third in the line of succession to the presidency.

The senator and Governor Buckingham, escorted by several of the leading men of Norwich, left that afternoon for Washington to render whatever service they could and to represent the state at the president's funeral services. The group included General Aiken, Colonel Hugh Henry Osgood, Joseph Selden, Henry Bell, Lorenzo Blackstone and Major J.B. Dennis.

When they arrived in Washington, they went to the White House, where Senator Foster introduced them to President Andrew Johnson. Governor Buckingham's biography described the scene as he shook the new president's hand and assured him of Connecticut's support. He was, it was noted, the first governor to do so.

In Norwich, although it was Easter Sunday and normally the most joyful of ecclesiastic feasts, the churches were draped in mourning, and the sermons took a decidedly sad and solemn tone.

LINCOLN'S FUNERAL

Mourners gathered in the East Room of the White House for the slain president's funeral service and then watched as his casket was brought to the rotunda of the Capitol. Senator Foster was among the honorary pallbearers. Connecticut's other senator, James Dixon, would be among the states' representatives escorting Lincoln's casket on the funeral train to the president's final resting place in Springfield, Illinois.

In Norwich, bells tolled throughout the day, and guns were fired every half hour. Black-trimmed flags flew at half-staff everywhere.

ANDERSONVILLE MEMORIAL

As 1866 began, George W. Smith was a man with a mission. On January 3, he left Norwich for the Andersonville Prison with the mission of claiming the bodies of the Norwich boys who died there. Smith was the U.S. assessor, according to that year's city directory. The city's patriotic fund financed his trip and the cost of shipping the coffins north.

In all, the bodies of nine Norwich soldiers known to have died at the prison were brought home. The *Norwich Aurora* reported on January 27 that Smith was bringing home the bodies of Joseph H. Winship, Sylvanus Downer, H.F. Champlin, E.F. Tisdale, William Hayward, James McDavid, Edward Blumley, William Davis and George W. Ward.

The funeral procession of President Abraham Lincoln on Pennsylvania Avenue in Washington. *Courtesy of the Library of Congress. LC-DIG-cwpb-00593.*

They were reburied on February 1, after a public memorial service at Breed Hall attended by many city residents. Afterward, a procession accompanied the flag-draped coffins as they were transported to Yantic Cemetery, where they were buried in a special section of the cemetery. The individual graves, marked by simple white stones, surround a thirty-pound Parrot rifle. Other graves were added later, continuing the circular arrangement in concentric circles. Each stone has the soldier's name, unit and date of death. The site is known as the Andersonville Memorial, a tribute to their patriotism and suffering. Norwich is acknowledged to be the first Northern city to recover its soldiers' bodies from the Andersonville Prison.

In 1906, the Connecticut General Assembly appropriated $6,000 for a monument representing Connecticut at the Andersonville National Cemetery. The seven-foot-tall bronze figure of a Union soldier was the

The Andersonville Memorial at Yantic Cemetery, Norwich, Connecticut. *Photo by Barry Wilson.*

creation of Norwich native Bela Lyon Pratt, a renowned sculptor at the turn of the twentieth century. A copy of the statue stands on the grounds of the state capitol building in Hartford.

SEDGWICK POST NO. 1, GAR

About a year after the war ended, some Union veterans in Decatur, Illinois, formed a fraternal organization that they called the Grand Army of the Republic (GAR) with their war experience the common bond among its members. The idea spread, and in February 1867, Connecticut's first GAR post was established in Norwich. Known as Sedgwick Post No. 1, it was named for General John Sedgwick of Cornwall, Connecticut, a well-beloved commander. General Sedgwick, who was called "Uncle John" by the men he commanded, was killed as he directed artillery placements at the Battle of Spotsylvania Courthouse in 1864. The first post commander was General William Aiken, who had been both a combat veteran and quartermaster general of Connecticut during the war.

The GAR became a powerful national political force, lobbying for veterans' pensions, voting rights for African American veterans and

Sedgwick Post No. 1. *Author's collection.*

other benefits, as well as establishment of Memorial Day (Decoration Day) as a national holiday. Presidential candidates sought GAR support, which was considered necessary to win the Republican nomination for the next forty years.

In its first years, the Sedgwick Post occupied rented rooms. Later, the group was able to acquire the Main Street home that had been Governor Buckingham's until his death.

THE SEVENTH REGIMENT VISITS NORWICH

Some observers called it the grandest social occasion Norwich had seen in the ten years since the city's 1859 bicentennial celebration. The dashing Seventh Regiment came up from New York to visit the Rose City. They were a New York militia unit that had been mustered into service during the war. Known as the "Silk Stocking" regiment or "Blue Bloods," the Seventh was known more for the socially-elite status of its members than its fighting prowess.

Norwich mayor J. Lloyd Greene extended an invitation for the regiment to come to Norwich on its annual field day. One of the New York papers whispered that the invitation was tendered at the behest of "an accomplished young lady of Norwich" who wanted to show off the regiment to which her fiancé belonged (and, presumably, the fiancé, who was never identified).

JULY 10, 1868, 5:00 A.M.

An artillery barrage went off, waking sleeping citizens and probably causing them to wonder if the war had started all over—until they remembered. Today, the Seventh Regiment comes to Norwich!

Then came the realization that the unit wasn't due for another hour, but since they had arrived, there was no time to lose. Houses were caught up in a flurry of activity—dressing for the morning's events, preparing food for an afternoon of callers, checking formalwear for the evening's grand ball.

Young boys (and probably girls) anticipated the parade, drill, uniforms and stories of the war. Older boys might be interested in the military aspects; perhaps for the older girls, thoughts went to the individual members of the regiment and dancing the night away. Norwich citizens might have caught a glimpse of members of the regiment as they walked around the city in the early hours to while away the time before the day's program began.

At the appointed hour, Mayor Lorenzo Blackstone welcomed the regiment with full military honors. Volunteers from two companies of the Connecticut National Guard Third Regiment served as an escort for the visiting regiment.

The day took on the air of a holiday as factories were closed, and the streets were filled with people eager to watch as the New York regiment and its escort marched along a rather circuitous route from downtown to Williams Park (now Chelsea Parade). Even the often-querulous *Norwich Aurora* was enthralled, describing the ranks of the Seventh as a sight "truly beautiful to behold" in their grey jackets and white pantaloons, with shining bayonets atop their rifles, a sharp contrast with the "dull blue" of the Connecticut militia uniforms.

Nearly every house along the line of the march was festooned in bunting with flags flying. Summer flowers were in bloom to beautify the grounds and show the city at its finest. A huge crowd was waiting at the park to watch the Seventh and the Connecticut units drill and pass in review before Mayor Blackstone.

A large tent had been erected on land near the park (probably where Park Congregational Church now stands). It was two hundred feet long, enough

Artist's rendering of the Seventh Regiment Ball. *Courtesy of the Slater Memorial Museum.*

to accommodate tables set for one thousand diners. The soldiers were served a splendid luncheon, and after more speeches, members of the regiment were dismissed to visit around the town.

Although it was an era that required a formal introduction before visiting someone's home, that rule was suspended for the day, and members of the regiment were welcomed by the city's leading citizens. The Seventh's regimental history noted, "Such hearty, generous and confiding hospitality was never known before and was long a fond remembrance."

Around 5:00 p.m., the regiment reassembled at the park for a dress review and then marched back to the steamer to rest and prepare for the evening's grand ball. In the intervening hours, the tent had been transformed into a "magnificent ball-room, brilliantly lighted, and elegantly and elaborately decorated. Crowded with beautiful women in elegant costumes, soldiers in gay uniforms, and citizens in full dress, the ball for the Seventh Regiment at Norwich was memorably successful." It was estimated that two thousand people enjoyed a brief concert followed by dancing.

The ball ended at midnight, when the men of the Seventh Regiment returned to their ship for the return voyage to New York.

A letter acknowledging the city's hospitality, signed by officers of the regiment, was framed and hung in city hall.

THE SOLDIERS' MONUMENT

By 1869, Governor Buckingham had become Senator Buckingham, but he still remained involved in local affairs. When talk about a suitable monument

Norwich Soldiers' Monument. *Author's collection.*

to the soldiers began, he was an early proponent, proposing formation of a committee to raise funds for a monument to honor those who died.

The chosen committee members were: Senator Buckingham, Amos W. Prentice, the Honorable John T. Wait, the Reverend Malcolm McGregor Dana, Dr. C.B. Webster, James S. Carew, Edwin P. Avery and E.P. Slocum. By a special motion, the town meeting added Eliza Greene and Eliza Perkins to the committee. At another a town meeting a year later, Buckingham introduced a resolution to provide funding for the monument.

The final design was for a twelve-foot-high soldier statue that would stand guard at the peak of Chelsea Parade where Broadway and Washington Street meet. It is believed to be the tallest soldier figure in the state. The statue stands on a fifteen-foot-high base of granite from the Batterson quarry in nearby Westerly, Rhode Island.

The monument was sculpted by Charles Conrad and constructed by Batterson, Canfield and Co. in Hartford. Its total cost was just over $16,000, including $2,200 for the brass plaques on the base. The monument was dedicated on April 23, 1875.

THE NORWICH MEMORIAL

Annals of Norwich

The monument committee also commissioned a soldiers' memorial volume. The committee finally prevailed on the Reverend Malcolm MacGregor Dana—pastor of Second Congregational Church and, later, the first pastor of Park Congregational Church—to do the extensive research needed and write the memorial volume "containing the military history of the town of Norwich during the exciting years of the war, recording its patriotism and sacrifices; memorializing the brave men who went forth from this community and yielded up their lives in the service of the country." Reverend Dana wrote:

> *In making our story public, we are but telling what part we took in the preservation of our National Union; what sacrifices were made among us for the suppression of a rebellion that threatened destruction to all our dearest rights.*
>
> *This by ourselves and by our children, will ever be a story which will be read with honest pride, and in the hope that it may deepen our love of country, and help us to remember with tender hearts the heroic dead, has this record of the patriotic services of the sons and daughters of Norwich been written.*

Bibliography

Berkey, J.M. "Winchester During the Civil War." *Encyclopedia Virginia*. Virginia Foundation for the Humanities, January 31, 2012. http://www.encyclopediavirginia.org/Winchester_During_the_Civil_War.

Buckingham, Samuel G.D.D. *The Life of William A. Buckingham: The War Governor of Connecticut, with a Review of His Public Acts, and Especially the Distinguished Services He Rendered His Country During the War of the Rebellion*. Springfield, MA: W.F. Adams Company, 1894. https://archive.org/details/buckinghamgov00buckrich.

Campbell, W.H.W. *Memorial Sketch of Lafayette S. Foster: United States Senator from Connecticut, and Acting Vice-President of the United States*. Boston, MA: Franklin Press; Rand, Avery, & Co., 1881.

Caulkins, Frances Manwaring. *History of Norwich, Connecticut: From Its Possession by the Indians to the Year 1866*. Chester, CT: Pequot Press, 1976.

Chapman, F.W. *The Buckingham Family; or, The Descendants of Thomas Buckingham, One of the First Settlers of Milford, Conn. Compiled at the Request of William A. Buckingham of Norwich, Conn*. Hartford, CT: Press of Case, Lockwood & Brainard, 1872. http://www.archive.org/stream/buckinghamfamily00inchap/buckinghamfamily00inchap_djvu.txt.

Croffut, William Augustus, and John M. Morris. *The Military and Civil History of Connecticut During the War of 1861–65*. New York: Ledyard Bill, 1868.

Dana, Malcolm McGregor. *The Norwich Memorial: The Annals of Norwich, New London County, Connecticut in the Great Rebellion of 1861–65*. Norwich, CT: J.H. Jewett and Company, 1873.

Farnsworth, Charles E. *Whirlwind and Storm: A Connecticut Cavalry Officer in the Civil War and Reconstruction*. Bloomington, IN: iUniverse, 2014.

Hurd, D. Hamilton. *History of New London County, with Biographical Sketches of Many of Its Pioneers and Prominent Men*. Philadelphia: J.W. Lewis & Co., 1882.

Lanman, Charles, ed. *Journal of Alfred Ely: A Prisoner of War in Richmond*. New York: D. Appleton and Company, 1862. https://archive.org/details/journalalfredel00lanmgoog.

Marshall, Benjamin Tinkham. *A Modern History of New London County*. Vols. 1–3. New York: Lewis Historical Company, 1922.

Page, Charles D. *History of the Fourteenth Regiment, Connecticut Volunteer Infantry*. Meriden, CT: Horton Printing Company, 1906. http://books.google.com/books?id=rwY0RR_tT0sC&source=gbs_navlinks_s.

Shelden, Rachel. *Washington Brotherhood: Politics, Social Life, and the Coming of the War*. Chapel Hill: University of North Carolina Press, 2013.

Walker, William C. *History of the Eighteenth Regiment Connecticut Volunteers in the War for the Union*. Norwich, CT: The Committee, 1885.

Zon, Calvin Goddard, ed. *The Good Fight that Didn't End: Henry P. Goddard's Account of Civil War and Peace*. Columbia: University of South Carolina Press, 2008.

Available at Otis Library Reference Department

Genealogical and Biographical Record of New London County, Connecticut. Chicago: J.H. Beers & Co., 1903.

Norwich newspapers, including the *Norwich Bulletin*, the *Norwich Aurora* and the *Norwich Courier*. 1800s–1900s.

Steadman's Norwich Directory. Norwich, CT: John W. Stedman Co., 1861–1900s.

Index

D

E

F

G

H

I

L

W

Y

About the Author

Photo by Stephanie Gallow.

Tricia Staley is a retired history teacher and school administrator. Prior to becoming an educator, she was a newspaper reporter, editor and advertising/public relations consultant. She majored in history at the University of Massachusetts–Amherst and holds a master's degree and sixth-year certificate from Sacred Heart University. She has also completed certificate programs in genealogy and maritime history. Tricia is president of Friends of the Slater Museum and on the board of Friends of the Otis Library in Norwich.

Norwich and the Civil War is her second book. Her first book, *Norwich in the Gilded Age: The Rose City's Millionaires' Triangle*, was published by The History Press in January 2014. An illustrated lecture and a popular walking tour are based on research for that book.

Tricia and her husband, Bob, live in Norwich with their dog, Fenway. They have two adult children.

Learn more on Facebook at Tricia Staley's Norwich History.